The Younger Australian POETS

M. Pirie

The Younger Australian POETS

Selected by Robert Gray & Geoffrey Lehmann

Hale & Iremonger

Typeset, printed & bound by
Southwood Press Pty Limited
80–92 Chapel Street, Marrickville, NSW

For the publisher
Hale & Iremonger Pty Limited
GPO Box 2552, Sydney, NSW

National Library of Australia Catalogue Card no. and
ISBN 0 86806 064 X (casebound)
ISBN 0 86806 065 8 (paperbound)

Published with the assistance of the
Literature Board of the Australia Council.

Contents

Introduction

Our purpose in compiling this anthology has been to discover what survives of Australia's so-called 'poetry explosion' of the 1970s. Such discovery, for the reading public, has been hindered by an unprecedented degree of factionalism among the poets, which has meant that two previous anthologies on this subject were entirely partisan.

The factionalism among the poets represented here has been, by Australian standards, unusually prolonged. During the 1940s, *Angry Penguins* died out very quickly, and the one or two outstanding 'Jindyworabak' poets were accepted without resistance into the general literary community. In the 1960s Vincent Buckley succeeded Douglas Stewart as the poetry editor of *The Bulletin,* which marked the ascendency of a younger group of Melbourne poets over an older group in Sydney. These two groups had different critical emphases, but shared certain basic criteria about the use of language. Although there were factions, the Australian literary community was able to accommodate and include new cohorts.

The 1970s have seen a very different sort of development. Some poets, such as Les Murray, quickly established a wide reputation. Murray, the most highly regarded poet in this anthology, is frequently prescribed for schools and universities, and he has some international standing. A number of other emerging poets were opposed to Australian literary influences, an opposition which has continued for more than a decade. Characterising themselves rather self-consciously as the 'generation of '68', they have, as a group (there are exceptions) rejected the validity of all Australian poetry which preceded their own. This goes much further than Vincent Buckley's opposition to the Sydney 'vitalists' in the 1960s: he did not reject Australian poetry outright. The most prominent figures of the 'generation of '68' have been John Tranter, Robert Adamson, Michael Dransfield (co-opted posthumously) and John Forbes.

A number of factors have affected this 1970s development. 'Modernism' (to use an old-fashioned term) arrived late in Australia. (It is striking that the poetic language of Douglas Stewart immediately became more traditional when he migrated from New Zealand to Australia. Traces of the British poets of the 1930s can be seen in his New Zealand poems, but these disappear with his arrival here.) Amongst Australian poets who had emerged by the 1950s, only Slessor and Webb, among the best writers, were really innovative, but Slessor had already stopped writing, and Webb was permanently confined to mental institutions. The pre-eminence of the Melbourne poets in the 1960s did nothing for innovation. The Melbourne poets, who were mainly literature academics, had a commitment to internationalism, but their poetry reproduced all that was grey and self-satisfied and excessively formal in the British 'Movement'. And whereas Larkin was understated and piercingly self-critical, much Melbourne poetry of the late fifties and the sixties fell into a parody of Yeatsian rhetoric.

The Australian poetic scene in the late 1960s was therefore viewed by most emerging poets as utterly dismal: not only was it unenlightened by recent American poetry, such as that of Bly, Simpson, Merwin, Snyder and O'Hara—it also avoided the renewing influence of earlier modernists like Stevens, Moore, Williams, Pound, and even Eliot. However, Slessor and Hart-Smith, to name only two of an earlier generation, had not been closed to influence in this way, and, therefore, not all of the newly emerging Australian poets had a totally depressed view of an Australian tradition. A number of those included here, who were not members of the 'generation of '68', were aware of the need to renovate and free poetic language in this country, but were also aware that the isolation of Australian poetry had given some of it an indigenous originality, and that there were things to be learned from and to admire in earlier confrontations with the uniqueness of the country. Certain earlier Australian poets' procedures might sometimes have been literary, but their work was often strong in content. A comparison of Judith Wright with, for instance, Stephen Spender, will support this contention. The Australian tradition has been concerned with the experience of a unique place, and such adjustment of awareness as this enforces has often led to a philosophical tough-mindedness. As well as Judith Wright, Slessor, Campbell and Fitzgerald come to mind.

The only older Australian poets to whom the 'generation of '68' felt they could relate were Bruce Beaver and Francis Webb. Beaver was appealing because of his receptiveness to recent American avant-gardists such as Frank O'Hara. Webb represented through his intuitive, obscure language, and in himself, alienation and an autonomous art. These younger poets did not respond to Bruce Dawe, although he was both opposed to the Vietnam war and neglectful of high culture, and at no stage (other than in a few peripheral poems) wrote in the 1960s Melbourne manner. The accessibility of Dawe's poetry and its insistent humanity and localism were evidently unsympathetic to them.

Perhaps because modernist innovation was deferred for such a long period in Australia, its emergence was marked by an unusual degree of division and abrasiveness (as well as fanfare). By no means was all the response from established poets negative: David Campbell and John Blight undertook marked changes of direction; the work of the established Melbourne poets loosened up considerably; and Rodney Hall and Thomas Shapcott, both recognised figures, were quick to establish themselves as the principal obstetricians for the emerging generation. Hall exercised this role over many years as poetry editor for *The Australian,* and Shapcott did so through his reviews, his influence as a member of the newly established Literature Board, and as editor of two large anthologies.

Personal factors also contributed to this polarisation among poets. Robert Adamson had initially been the protégé of Roland Robinson, a well-known poet and editor of *Poetry* magazine, the journal of the then active Poetry Society of Australia. But later Robinson was, in effect, expelled by a group associated with Adamson, and *Poetry* became *New Poetry,* and the leading organ for the 'generation of '68'. The bitterness and disaffection resulting from this event were compounded by the style of the magazine, which was anti-intellectual and erratic.

Poetry Australia, a magazine controlled by the poet and medical practitioner Grace Perry, had broken away from *Poetry* at the time when Roland Robinson became editor and there was a continuing feud between the two journals. While it was edited by Dr Perry herself, *Poetry Australia* was quite sympathetic to the emerging poets, and she was responsible for publishing John Tranter's first book, as an issue of her magazine, which gave it a very wide circulation. Then, for a number of years, until 1981, Dr Perry allowed Les Murray to become the effective editor, and Murray was much less receptive to the 'generation of '68'. Thus the rivalry between the magazines continued.

As an editor, Murray had a very distinctive and consistent style. A group of still newer poets including Kevin Hart, Alan Gould, Mark O'Connor, Jamie Grant, Andrew Sant and Peter Kocan, began to appear regularly in the magazine, along with the more established figures like Geoffrey Lehmann, Roger McDonald, Rhyll McMaster, Robert Gray and Geoff Page; and Murray was very generous to those whose poetry he liked. His dislikes were equally definite: he was cool to the work of Bruce Beaver, and antipathetic to all the 'generation of '68', except for certain modes in John Forbes's work—he saw their poetic as, at its best, élitist and the product of an Americanised aculturalisation.

In all this, a clear division cannot be made between so-called avant-gardists and leftists on the one side and conservatives and establish-mentarians on the other. For instance, Murray is far more populist in his subject-matter and attitudes than his opponents, but he was also one of the few Australian poets unopposed to the Vietnam war. And few of those who write in an inverted, deliberately amoral and non-communicative style, while at the same time claiming to be leftists and radicals, have been so actively involved in politics as, for instance, Geoff Page has been with the Labor Party. Tim Thorne and Nigel Roberts, amongst the poets in John Tranter's *The New Australian Poetry,* were directly involved in the anti-Vietnam moratoriums, but the large-scale protests by poets against the war were organised and carried off by so-called establishment figures like Fitzgerald and Campbell.

The contention of the 'generation of '68' that they are the ex-perimentalists, the avant-garde, is based on their having appropriated wholesale an established, anthologised American style of writing — that of the New York school. This in turn is directly derivative of early-modernist French poetry (see the works of Pierre Reverdy, and of Apollinaire, in particular 'Zone'). On the Australians' part, this was hardly the most daring, inventive and exploratory of directions to take.

It is misleading of the 'generation of '68' to claim that they represent modernism: at best, they only represent one specific stream of modernism, that from the French symbolists, to the surrealists, to the New York abstractionists like Ashbery, Berrigan and O'Hara. And this, it might be argued, if modernity is to be the issue, is not the most modern of modernisms, since the Poundian variety was a criticism of that whole, essentially symbolist, aesthetic. The division in modern poetry is really between what might be called abstractionist and precisionist attitudes to language—both of which can claim to belong to the modern period. In technique, the 'generation of '68' are certainly no more innovative than some of their opponents, particularly considering their employment of the sonnet form.

In making selections for this anthology we have chosen only those poets who we feel can manage a precise, communicative use of language and who have something moving or interesting to say. We have looked for, along with literary values, whatever impressed us as human ones; but the literary values have not been the less important—on the contrary, there is no literature without them. The essence of an anti-humanist position is solipsism, in its varying degrees; it can appear not only stylistically, but also as an intellectual pleasure in cruelty. We have rejected this aggression towards the subject-matter and the reader; it has long been identified as reverse sentimentalism, and we have wanted to avoid sentimentality of all varieties (which is something more than a purely literary judgement).

Given these criteria, an even slightly knowledgeable reader will be able to understand the assessments made here, the unconventional choices and the exclusions.

We have not included any abstractionist poems because of doubts about the motivation behind such writing: the genre seems to us so obviously reductive. It is apparent from the valedictory tone of the introduction to *The New Australian Poetry* that boredom with such limitations has (belatedly) descended on even the practitioners of the style.

It should be mentioned that competition between poets has been exaggerated by an economic factor. The funding of writers by the Australia Council through direct grants, and the availability of writer-in-residence positions now make it feasible to be a professional poet, in a way never before possible, if this income can be supplemented by a little part-time journalism, teaching, and so on. It is a precarious existence, but a number of poets live regularly in this manner, and the intensity of competition for the privilege has become Darwinian.

In compiling this anthology, we have not attempted to be sociologically representative. Our sole criterion has been the quality of individual poems. These have had to sustain interest at all levels of response: technically and emotionally. Each of us has retained a right of veto, and sometimes we disagreed, but we do not believe that, at present, rigour is what is most harmful. We believe the opposite approach has alienated the reading public, who have found the newspapers, literary journals and bookshops flooded with poetry that is semi-literate, pretentious, obscure, silly or vicious. There was nothing uniquely bad about the poetry of the 1970s, since most poetry written anywhere, at any time, is forgettable, but we wanted to counter the notion that it is easier and more self-indulgent to write poetry than fiction or good prose, and that poetry is less rewarding to the reader. Our concern, often at the cost of personal loyalties, has been to produce a book which disregards partisan lines, and in which the reader can find both insight and enjoyment.

LES A. MURRAY (b. 1938)

As a child Les Murray lived on a dairy farm at Bunyah, on the north coast of New South Wales. Later he studied arts at Sydney University. He now lives in Sydney, but frequently returns to the country to renew contact with the main source of his verse.

Murray has been the most widely acclaimed Australian poet since Slessor and Wright; many see him as the writer who maintains the traditions of Australian poetry. A poem such as 'Driving through sawmill towns' is a continuation of the landscape tradition of these two poets, but also contains an element of 'interiorisation' which suggests the early work of the American poet Robert Bly. In the same way, 'The Princes' land' combines Slessor's urbane and ornate mode with an even more noticeable influence from the classicising style of the American Louis Simpson. Despite these antecedents, both poems are original in subject-matter and tone.

The simplicity of Murray's early poems contrasts with his increasingly dense and baroque language. Murray is anti-élitist and addresses the common reader, but uses the language of high art out of a refusal to compromise his talent, or the complexity of his subject, and out of optimism about the responsiveness of his audience to poems which articulate their lives.

A measure of Murray's importance as a poet is his ability to encompass an encyclopaedic range of subject-matter, which is matched by his range of forms. Unlike predecessors such as Hope, he writes both an accomplished villanelle and brilliant free verse. As well as his poems about the country and the immemorial dependence of man on cattle and the earth, he can employ the Spenserian stanza so that it lights up like an electronic console, with his admiration for machinery and the space age, as in 'Machine portraits with pendant spaceman'.

Murray's subject might be identified as the necessity to maintain traditional values while accepting technological progress. But the values he favours are those that many see as most in need of transcending or refining: a polarisation of male and female roles, an ultramontane Catholic opposition to social meliorists, a romanticising of the supposed military virtues. Murray's disparagers are inclined to ignore his ability to speak sympathetically from many viewpoints: those of migrants, aborigines, underdogs, police and even city-dwellers.

Driving through sawmill towns

1

In the high cool country,
having come from the clouds,
down a tilting road
into a distant valley,
you drive without haste. Your windscreen parts the forest,
swaying and glancing, and jammed midday brilliance
crouches in clearings . . .
then you come across them,
the sawmill towns, bare hamlets built of boards
with perhaps a store,
perhaps a bridge beyond
and a little sidelong creek alive with pebbles.

2

The mills are roofed with iron, have no walls:
you look straight in as you pass, see lithe men working,
the swerve of a winch,
dim dazzling blades advancing
through a trolley-borne baulk
till it sags apart
in a manifold sprawl of weatherboards and battens.

The men watch you pass:
when you stop your car and ask them for directions,
tall youths look away—
it is the older men who
come out in blue singlets and talk softly to you.

Beside each mill, smoke trickles out of mounds
of ash and sawdust.

3

You glide on through town,
your mudguards damp with cloud.
The houses there wear verandahs out of shyness,
all day in calendared kitchens, women listen
for cars on the road,
lost children in the bush,
a cry from the mill, a footstep—
nothing happens.

The half-heard radio sings
its song of sidewalks.

Sometimes a woman, sweeping her front step,
or a plain young wife at a tankstand fetching water
in a metal bucket will turn round and gaze
at the mountains in wonderment,
looking for a city.

4

Evenings are very quiet. All around
the forest is there.
As night comes down, the houses watch each other:
a light going out in a window here has meaning.

You speed away through the upland,
glare through towns
and are gone in the forest, glowing on far hills.

On summer nights
ground-crickets sing and pause.
In the dark of winter, tin roofs sough with rain,
downpipes chafe in the wind, agog with water.
Men sit after tea
by the stove while their wives talk, rolling a dead match
between their fingers,
thinking of the future.

The princes' land

for Valerie, on her birthday

Leaves from the ancient forest gleam
In the meadow brook, and dip, and pass.
Six maidens dance on the level green,
A seventh toys with an hourglass,

Letting fine hours sink away,
Turning to sift them back again.
An idle prince, with a cembalo,
Sings to the golden afternoon.

Two silver knights, met in a wood,
Tilt at each other, clash and bow.
Upon a field semé of birds
Tom Bread-and-Cheese sleeps by his plough.

But now a deadly stillness comes
Upon the brook, upon the green,
Upon the seven dancing maids,
The dented knights are dulled to stone.

The hours in the hourglass
Are stilled to fine fear, and the wood

To empty burning. Tom the hind
Walks in his sleep in pools of blood. . . .

The page we've reached is grey with pain.
Some will not hear, some run away,
Some go to write books of their own,
Some few, as the tale grows cruel, are gay.

But we who have no other book
Spell out the gloomy, blazing text,
Page by slow page, wild year by year,
Our hope refined to what comes next,

And yet attentive to each child
Who says he's looked ahead and seen
How the tale will go, or spied
A silver page two pages on,

For, as the themes knit and unfold,
Somewhere far on, where all is changed,
Beyond all twists of grief and fear,
We look to glimpse that land again:

The brook descends in music through
The meadows of that figured land,
Nine maidens from the ageless wood
Move in their circles, hand in hand.

Two noble figures, counterchanged,
Fence with swift passion, pause and bow.
All in a field impaled with sun
The Prince of Cheese snores by his plough.

Watching bright hours file away,
Turning to sift them back again,
The Prince of Bread, with a cembalo
Hums to the golden afternoon.

The ballad trap

In the hanging gorges
the daring compact wears thin,
picking meat from small skeletons,
counting damp notes in a tin,

the rifle birds ringing at noon
in the steep woods,
hard-riding boys dazed at the brink
of their attitudes,

the youngest wheedling for songs,
his back to the night,
dark mountains the very English
for souring delight:

Remember the Escort? Remember. . .
lamps long ago
and manhood filched from the horse police
and a name from Cobb and Co.

Their metre hobbled, the horses
hump their dark life,
longing for marriage, the tall man
sharpens his knife —

Yes, let us sing! cries the Captain
while we have breath.
Better, God knows, than this thinking.
The ballad ends with their death.

Birds in their title work freeholds of straw

At the hour I slept
kitchen lamps were sending out barefoot children
muzzy with stars and milk thistles
stoning up cows.

They will never forget their quick-fade cow-piss slippers
nor chasing such warmth over white frost, saffron to steam.
It will make them sad bankers.

It may subtly ruin them for clerks
this deeply involved unpickable knot of feeling
for the furred, smeared flesh of creation, the hate, the
    concern
Viciously, out of sight, they pelt cows with stove-lengths
and hit them with pipes,
and older brothers sometimes, in more frenzied guilt,
have rancid, cracked eyes.
The city man's joke doesn't stretch to small minotaur bones.

But strange to think, as the dairy universe
reels from a Wall Street tremor, a London red-shift
on the flesh-eating graphs
and no longer only the bright and surplus children
get out of these hills,
how ghostly cows must be crowding the factory floors now
and licking black turbines
for the spectral salt
till the circuit-breaker's stunning greenhide crack
sears all but wages.

o

In the marginal dialect of this valley
(Agen my son grows up, tourists won't hear it)
udders are *elders.*

It was very bad news for the Kirk:
old men of the hard grey cloth, their freckled faces
distended, squeezing grace through the Four Last Things
in a Sabbath bucket.
I can tell you sparetime childhoods force-fed this
make solid cheese, but often strangely veined.
I'm thinking of aunts who had telescopes to spot

pregnancies, inside wedlock or out
(there is no life more global than a village)
and my father's uncles, monsters of hospitality.

Perhaps we should forget the seven-day-week tinned bucket
and the little children dead beat at their desks
Caesar got up and Milked then he Got his soldiers—
but birds in their title work freeholds of straw
and the eagle his of sky.

Dripstone for Caesar.

The pure food act

Night, as I go into the place of cattle.

Night over the dairy
the strainers sleeping in their fractions,
vats
and the mixing plunger, that dwarf ski-stock, hung.

On the creekstone cement
water driven hard through the Pure Food Act
dries slowest round tree-segment stools,
each buffed
to a still bum-shine,
sides calcified with froth.

Country disk-jocks
have the idea. Their listeners aren't all human.
Cows like, or let their milk for, a firm beat
nothing too plangent (diesel bass is good)
Sinatra, though, could calm a yardful of horns
and the Water Music
has never yet corrupted honest milkers
in their pure food act.

The quiet dismissal switching it off, though,
and carrying the last bucket, saline-sickly
still undrinkable raw milk to pour in high
for its herringbone and cooling pipe-grid
fall
to the muscle-building cans.

His wedding, or a war
might excuse a man from milking
but milk-steeped hands are good for a violin
and a cow in rain time is
a stout wall of tears.

But I'm britching back.

I let myself out through the bail gate.
Night, as I say.
Night, as I go out to the place of cattle.

The breach

I am a policeman
it is easier to make me seem an oaf
than to handle the truth

I came from a coaldust town
when I was seventeen, because there was nothing
for a young fellow there

the Force drew me because of a sense I had
and have grown out of

I said to Ware once, Harry, you're the best
cop of the lot: you only arrest falls
he was amused

I seem to be making an inventory of my life
but in that house opposite, first floor
there is a breach
and me, in this body I am careful with,
I'm going to have to enter that house soon
and stop that breach
it is a bad one people could fall through
we know that three have
and he's got a child poised

I have struck men in back rooms late at night
with faces you could fall a thousand feet down
and I've seen things in bowls

the trick is not to be a breach yourself
and to stop your side from being one
I suppose

the sniper Spiteri, when I was just out of cadets—
some far-west cockies' boys straight off the sheep train
came up with their .303s and offered to help
they were sixteen years old

we chased them away, not doubting for a minute
they could do what they said
bury your silver the day we let that start

now I've said my ideals

Snowy cut, snow he cut . . .
A razor-gang hood my uncle claims he met
is running through my mind
in Woolloomooloo, wet streets, the nineteen twenties
dear kind Snowy Cutmore

Snowy cuts no more
he was a real breach

also, in our town, I
remember the old hand bowsers, that gentle apop-
poplexy of benzine in the big glass heads
twenty years since I saw them

There's a moment with every man who has started a stir
(even this kind, who'd lap up prayer and fasting)

when he tires of it, wants to put it aside
and be back, unguilty, that morning, pouring the milk

that is the time to separate him from it
if I am very good I'll judge that time
just about right

the ideal is to keep the man and stop
the breach
that's the high standard

but the breach must close

if later goes all right
I am going to paint the roof of our house
on my day off.

Ware: Special Sgt. Harry Ware (1897-1970) founder and first officer-in-charge of
N.S.W. Police Cliff Rescue Squad.

Portrait of the autist as a new world driver

A car is also
a high-speed hermitage. Here
only the souls of policemen can get at you.
Who would put in a telephone,
that merciless foot-in-the-door
of realities, realties?

Delight of a stick-shift—
farms were abandoned for these pleasures. Second
to third in this Mazda is a stepped inflection
third back to first at the lights
a concessive
V of junction.

Under the overcoming
undiminishing sky you are scarcely supervised:
you can let out language
to exercise, to romp in the grass beyond Greek.
You can rejoice in tongues,
orotate parafundities.

    They simplify
    who say the Artist's a child
    they miss the point closely: an artist
    even if he has brothers, sisters, spouse
    is an only child.

    Among the self-taught
    the loners, chart-freaks, bush encyclopedists
    there are protocols, too: we meet
    gravely as stiff princes, and swap fact:
    did you know some bats can climb side on?

    Mind you, Hitler was one of us.
    He had a theory. We also count stern scholars
    in whose disputes you almost hear the teenage
    hobbyist still disputing proof and mint
    and wheelmen who murmur *Suffering is bourgeois.*

But swapping cogs to pass a
mountainous rig and its prime mover, I
reflect that driving's a mastery the mastered
are holding on to.
It has gone down among the ancient crafts
to hide in our muscles.

Indeed, if you asked
where the New World is, I'd have to answer
he is in his car
he is booming down the highways
in that funnel of blue-green-gold, tree-flecked and streaming
light that a car is always breaking out of—

we didn't come of
the New World. But we've owned it.
From a steady bang, ever more globes, flying outward.
Strange tunings are between us.
Of course we love our shells: they make the anthill
bearable. Of course the price is blood.

The broad bean sermon

Beanstalks, in any breeze, are a slack church parade
without belief, saying *trespass against us* in unison,
recruits in mint Air Force dacron, with unbuttoned leaves.

Upright with water like men, square in stem-section
they grow to great lengths, drink rain, keel over all ways,
kink down and grow up afresh, with proffered new greenstuff.

Above the cat-and-mouse floor of a thin bean forest
snails hang rapt in their food, ants hurry through several
    dimensions,
spiders tense and sag like little black flags in their cordage.

Going out to pick beans with the sun high as fence-tops, you
    find
plenty, and fetch them. An hour or a cloud later
you find shirtfulls more. At every hour of daylight

appear more that you missed: ripe, knobbly ones, fleshy-sided,
thin-straight, thin-crescent, frown-shaped, bird-shouldered,
      boat-keeled ones,
beans knuckled and single-bulged, minute green dolphins at
      suck,

beans upright like lecturing, outstretched like blessing fingers
in the incident light, and more still, oblique to your notice
that the noon glare or cloud-light or afternoon slants will
      uncover

till you ask yourself Could I have overlooked so many, or
do they form in an hour? unfolding into reality
like templates for subtly broad grins, like unique caught
      expressions,

like edible meanings, each sealed around with a string
and affixed to its moment, an unceasing colloquial assembly,
the portly, the stiff, and those lolling in pointed green
      slippers. . . .

Wondering who'll take the spare bagfulls, you grin with
      happiness
—it is your health—you vow to pick them all
even the last few, weeks off yet, misshapen as toes.

from **The Buladelah-Taree Holiday Song Cycle**

6

Barbecue smoke is rising at Legge's Camp; it is steaming into the
      midday air,
all around the lake shore, at the Broadwater, it is going up
      among the paperbark trees,

a heat-shimmer of sauces, rising from tripods and flat steel, at
that place of the Cone-shells,
at that place of the Seagrass, and the tiny segmented things
swarming in it, and of the Pelican.
Dogs are running around disjointedly; water escapes from their
mouths,
confused emotions from their eyes; humans snarl at them
Gwanout and Hereboy, not varying their tone much;
the impoverished dog people, suddenly sitting down to nuzzle
themselves; toddlers side with them:
toddlers, running away purposefully at random, among cars,
into big drownie-water (come back, Cheryl-Ann!).
They rise up as charioteers, leaning back on the tow-bar; all their
attributes bulge at once;
swapping swash shoulder-wings for the white-sheeted shoes that
bear them.
they are skidding over the flat glitter, stiff with grace, for once
not travelling to arrive.
From the high dunes over there, the rough blue distance, at
length they come back behind the boats,
and behind the boats' noise, cartwheeling, or sitting down, into
the lake's warm chair;
they wade ashore and eat with the families, putting off that
uprightness, that assertion,
eating with the families who love equipment, and the freedom
from equipment,
with the fathers who love driving, and lighting a fire between
stones.

13

The stars of the holiday step out all over the sky.
People look up at them, out of their caravan doors and their
campsites;

people look up from the farms, before going back; they gaze at
their year's worth of stars.

The Cross hangs head-downward, out there over Markwell;

it turns upon the Still Place, the pivot of the Seasons, with one
shoulder rising:

'Now I'm beginning to rise, with my Pointers and my Load . . .'

hanging eastwards, it shines on the sawmills and the lakes, on
the glasses of the Old People.

Looking at the Cross, the galaxy is over our left shoulder, slung
up highest in the east;

there the Dog is following the Hunter; the Dog Star pulsing
there above Forster; it shines down on the Bikies,

and on the boat-hire sheds, there at the place of the Oyster; the
place of the Shark's Eggs and her Hide;

the Pleiades are pinned up high on the darkness, away back
above the Manning;

they are shining on the Two Blackbutt Trees, on the rotted river
wharves, and on the towns;

standing there, above the water and the lucerne flats, at the place
of the Families;

their light sprinkles down on Taree of the Lebanese shops, it
mingles with the streetlights and their glare.

People recover the starlight, hitching north,

travelling north beyond the seasons, into that country of the
Communes, and of the Banana:

the Flying Horse, the Rescued Girl, and the Bull, burning
steadily above that country.

Now the New Moon is low down in the west, that remote
direction of the Cattlemen,

and of the Saleyards, the place of steep clouds, and of the Rodeo;

the New Moon who has poured out her rain, the moon of the
Planting-times.

People go outside and look at the stars, and at the melon-rind
moon,

the Scorpion going down into the mountains, over there towards
Waukivory, sinking into the tree-line,

in the time of the Rockmelons, and of the Holiday . . .

the Cross is rising on his elbow, above the glow of the horizon;
carrying a small star in his pocket, he reclines there brilliantly,
above the Alum Mountain, and the lakes threaded on the Myall
     River, and above the Holiday.

Immigrant voyage

My wife came out on the *Goya*
in the mid-year of our century.

In the fogs of that winter
many hundred ships were sounding;
the DP camps were being washed to sea.

The bombsites and the ghettoes
were edging out to Israel,
to Brazil, to Africa, America.

The separating ships were bound away
to the cities of refuge
built for the age of progress.

Hull-down and pouring light
the tithe-barns, the cathedrals
were bearing the old castes away.

        O
Pattern-bombed out of babyhood,
Hungarians-become-Swiss,
the children heard their parents:
Argentina? Or Australia?
Less politics, in Australia . . .

Dark Germany, iron frost
and the waiting many weeks
then a small converted warship
under the moon, turning south.

Way beyond the first star
and beyond Cap Finisterre
the fishes and the birds
did eat of their heave-offerings.

O

The *Goya* was a barracks:
mess-queue, spotlights, tower,
crossing the Middle Sea.

In the haunted blue light
that burned nightlong in the sleeping-decks
the tiered bunks were restless
with coughing, demons, territory.

On the Sea of Sweat, the Red Sea,
the flat heat melted even
dulled deference of the injured.
Nordics and Slavonics
paid salt-tax day and night, being
absolved of Europe

but by the Gate of Tears
the barrack was a village
with accordions and dancing
(Fräulein, kennen Sie meinen Rhythmus?)
approaching the southern stars.

O

Those who said Europe
has fallen to the Proles
and the many who said
we are going for the children,

the nouveau poor
and the cheerful shirtsleeve Proles,
the children, who thought
No Smoking signs meant men
mustn't dress for dinner,

those who had hopes
and those who knew that they
were giving up their lives

were becoming the people
who would say, and sometimes urge,
in the English-speaking years:
we came out on the *Goya*.

O
At last, a low coastline,
old horror of Dutch sail-captains.

Behind it, still unknown,
sunburnt farms, strange trees, family jokes
and all the classes of equality.

As it fell away northwards
there was one last week for songs,
for dreaming at the rail,
for beloved meaningless words.

Standing in to Port Phillip
in the salt-grey summer light
the village dissolved
into strained shapes holding luggage;

now they, like the dour
Australians below them, were facing
encounter with the Foreign
where all subtlety fails.

O

Those who, with effort,
with concealment, with silence, had resisted
the collapsed star Death,
who had clawed their families from it,
those crippled by that gravity

were suddenly, shockingly
being loaded aboard lorries:
They say, another camp—
One did not come for this—

As all the refitted
ships stood, oiling, in the Bay,
spectres, furious and feeble,
accompanied the trucks through Melbourne,

resignation, understandings
that cheerful speed dispelled at length.

That first day, rolling north
across the bright savanna,
not yet people, but numbers.
Population. Forebears.

O

Bonegilla, Nelson Bay,
the dry-land barbed wire ships
from which some would never land.

In these, as their parents
learned the Fresh Start music:
physicians nailing crates,
attorneys cleaning trams,
the children had one last
ambiguous summer holiday.

Ahead of them lay
the Deep End of the schoolyard,
tribal testing, tribal soft-drinks,
and learning English fast,
the Wang-Wang language.

Ahead of them, refinements:
thumbs hooked down hard under belts
to repress gesticulation;

ahead of them, epithets:
wog, reffo, Commo Nazi,
things which can be forgotten
but must first be told.

And farther ahead
in the years of the Coffee Revolution
and the Smallgoods Renaissance,
the early funerals:

the misemployed, the unadaptable,
those marked by the Abyss,

friends who came on the *Goya*
in the mid-year of our century.

Machine portraits with pendant spaceman

for Valerie

The bulldozer stands short as a boot on its heel-high ripple
        soles;
it has toecapped stumps aside all day, scuffed earth and
        trampled rocks
making a hobnailed dyke downstream of raw clay shoals.

Its work will hold water. The man who bounced high on the
        box
seat, exercising levers, would swear a full frontal orthodox
oath to that. First he shaved off the grizzled scrub
with that front end safety razor supplied by the school of hard
        knocks
then he knuckled down and ground his irons properly; they
        copped many a harsh rub.
At knock-off time, spilling thunder, he surfaced like a sub.

                    O

Speaking of razors, the workshop amazes with its strop,
its elapsing leather drive belt angled to the slapstick flow
of fast work in the Chaplin age; tightened, it runs like syrup,
streams like a mill-sluice, fiddles like a glazed virtuoso.
With the straitlaced summary cut of Sam Brownes long ago
it is the last of the drawn lash and bullocking muscle
left in engineering. It's where the panther leaping, his swift
        shadow
and all such free images turned plastic. Here they dwindle,
        dense with oil,
like a skein between tough factory hands, pulley and Diesel.

                    O

Shaking in slow low flight, with its span of many jets,
the combine seeder at nightfall swimming over flat land
is a style of machinery we'd imagined for the fictional planets:
in the high glassed cabin, above vapour-pencilling floodlights,
        a hand,
gloved against the cold, hunts along the medium-wave band
for company of Earth voices; it crosses speech garble music—
the Brandenburg Conch the Who the Illyrian High Com-
        mand—
as seed wheat in the hoppers shakes down, being laced into
        the thick
night-dampening plains soil, and the stars waver out and stick.

O

Flags and a taut fence discipline the mountain pasture
where giant upturned mushrooms gape mildly at the sky
catching otherworld pollen. Poppy-smooth or waffle-ironed,
        each armature
distils wild and white sound. These, Earth's first antennae
tranquilly angled outwards, to a black, not a gold infinity,
swallow the millionfold numbers that print out as a risen
glorious Apollo. They speak control to satellites in high
bursts of algorithm. And some of them are tuned to win
answers to fair questions, viz. What is the Universe in?

O

How many metal-bra and trumpet-flaring film extravaganzas
underlie the progress of the space shuttle's Ground Trans-
        porter Vehicle
across concrete-surfaced Florida? Atop oncreeping house-high
        panzers,
towering drydock and ocean-liner decks, there perches a
        gridiron football
field in gradual motion; it is the god-platform; it sustains the
        bridal
skyscraper of liquid Cool, and the rockets borrowed from the
        Superman
and the bricked aeroplane of Bustout-and-return, all vertical,
conjoined and myth-huge, approaching the starred gantry
        where human
lightning will crack, extend, and vanish upwards from this
        caravan.

O

Gold-masked, the foetal warrior
unslipping on a flawless floor,
I backpack air; my life machine
breathes me head-Earthwards, speaks the Choctaw
of tech-talk that earths our discipline—

but the home world now seems outside-in;
I marvel that here background's so fore
and sheathe my arms in the unseen

a dream in images unrecalled
from any past takes me   I soar
at the heart of fall on a drifting line

this is the nearest I have been
to oneness with the everted world
the unsinking leap   the stone unfurled

O

In a derelict village picture show I will find a projector,
dust-matted, but with film in its drum magazines, and the lens
mysteriously clean. The film will be called *Insensate Violence*,
no plot, no characters, just shoot burn scream beg claw
bayonet trample brains — I will hit the reverse switch then, in
    conscience,
and the thing will run backwards, unlike its coeval the
    machinegun;
blood will unspill, fighters lift and surge apart; horror will be
    undone
and I will come out to a large town, bright parrots round the
    saleyard pens
and my people's faces healed of a bitter sophistication.

O

The more I act, the stiller I become;
the less I'm lit, the more spellbound my crowd;
I accept all colours, and with a warming hum
I turn them white and hide them in a cloud.
To give long life is a power I'm allowed
by my servant, Death. I am what you can't sell
at the world's end — and if you're still beetle-browed
try some of my treasures: an adult bird in its shell
or a pink porker in his own gut, Fritz the Abstract Animal.

O

No riddles about a crane. This one drops a black clanger on
        cars
and the palm of its four-thumbed steel hand is a raptor of
        wrecked tubing;
the ones up the highway hoist porridgy concrete, long spars
and the local skyline; whether raising aloft on a string
bizarre workaday angels, or letting down a rotating
man on a sphere, these machines are inclined to maintain
a peace like world war, in which we turn over everything
to provide unceasing victories. Now the fluent lines stop, and
        strain
engrosses this tower on the frontier of junk, this crane.

O

Before a landscape sprouts those giant stepladders that pump
        oil
or before far out iron mosquitoes attach to the sea
there is this sortilege with phones that plug into mapped soil,
the odd gelignite bump to shake trucks, paper scribbling out
        serially
as men dial Barrier Reefs long enfolded beneath the geology
or listen for black Freudian beaches; they seek a miles-wide
        pustular
rock dome of pure Crude, a St. Pauls-in-profundis. There are
        many
wrong numbers on the geophone, but it's brought us some
        distance — and by car.
Every machine has been love and a true answer.

O

Not a high studded ship boiling cauliflower under her keel
nor a ghost in bootlaced canvas — just a length of country road
afloat between two shores, winding wet wire rope reel-to-reel,
dismissing romance sternwards. Six cars and a hay truck are her
        load

plus a thoughtful human cast which could, in some dramatic
    episode,
become a world. All machines in the end join God's creation
growing bygone, given, changeless — but a river ferry has its
    timeless mode
from the grinding reedy outset; it enforces contemplation.
We arrive. We traverse depth in thudding silence. We go on.

GEOFFREY LEHMANN (b. 1940)

Born in Sydney, Geoffrey Lehmann worked for a number of years as a
solicitor. He is now a university lecturer in tax and law.

Most of his early poetry adheres to iambic pentameter, but with
Ross's Poems the rhythms and tone are more free-ranging and exploratory. From his earliest work he has used the persona, and even the
poems written in his own voice often focus on another person.

The poems in the book *Ross's Poems* are spoken through the voice of
an actual person, a farmer living on the western slopes of New South
Wales. Many (though not all) of the experiences are Ross's, but the
interpretations and values drawn from them are the author's own.
Nero's Poems appeared after *Ross's Poems,* but the period of com-
position of the books overlapped. They may be seen as complementary
aspects of the same personality. Ross lives within the restrictions of
family, countryside and weather; Nero is essentially urban and wants to
make the world an extension of his own imagination.

Lehmann's direct language has perhaps been influenced by Cavafy
and Arthur Waley. The explicit treatment of subject-matter and the
painstaking accumulation of factual detail in his poems sometimes leads
to a drabness in their rhythm. His work expresses various aspects of a
liberal humanist and sceptical viewpoint.

Pieces for my father

I

My father did not like the Swedish vases
Of blue and purple glass I bought to grace
The mantelpiece and elegantly gleam
Down on his bed, pure elongated shapes
Of blown glass with round bowls and long thin necks.
'Rubbish!' he said, resenting change and took
Them down and seized with a divine zest
(And also guilty, trying to laugh it off)
Grunting set up assorted whisky, wine
And brandy bottles on the mantelpiece,
A sherry bottle as the crowning piece
Set on a clock, to gurgle through the night
And phosphoresce and permeate his dreams
With cobwebbed cellars, great vats, musty barrels. . . .

II

It's spring and children in their billy-carts
Roar down the hill, chalk dirty words on footpaths,
And birds perched on electric wires are trilling,
While breezes from the bright blue harbour buffet
A gnarled branch green with buds.
                              Ka-dell! Ka-dell!
The ice-cream man drives slowly past and rings
His bell. But in his tool-room my old father
Rummaging in old boxes thick with sawdust
Extracts an ancient bell with tinny tone
And chuckling runs into his yard and rings it.
Ka-dell! Ka-dell! And so bell answers bell.
'Ha! Ha! He thinks that he's got competition.
See, now he's going!' laughs my father proudly.
It's spring and children in their billy-carts
Are shouting while a child of seventy
With balding pate is ringing an old bell.

III

Silence of night and only possums scuttling.
The house asleep but for my studious self
And my old father with his eyeglass peering
Into his twinkling galaxies of watches,
Time spawned like stardust in their shimmering wheels.
Rising, he takes his eyeglass out and comes
Across to me. An old man's heavy breathing.
Shyly he lifts his frayed and faded shirt.
'D'you see it son? A tick.'
                              Sweet smell of sweat
And flabby, freckled back.
                              A patch of red,
A small black kicking head for which I probe
With tweezers. A sharp jerk. My father winces.
I go back to my book and now my father
Browses once more amongst his countless watches,
The spinning stardust of their endless wheels.

IV

On his sore ageing legs my father rubs
Rose embrocation from an old brown bottle,
And the hot dusk and the grave sticky scent
Put me in mind of childhood holidays,
Mosquitoes, citronella, sleepless nights,
Queensland and the gruff trains that slowly jerked us
Past moonlit canefields and crawled over bridges.
And still I see those brown-cream butterflies circling
While a cat leapt to catch them in the sun,
The scabs upon my legs from sandfly bites,
My father laughing as I ran from wasps
And photographing various island scenes
And waves bright as the wings of whirring beetles.
Rose embrocation and its swarming scent,
And I would hold my father here against
The window blue with dusk for ever.
Night folds us in and stings us with her stars.

A poem for Maurice O'Shea

for Garry Shead

It is wine-harvest, summer, the year's heart.
At night the vines bend on their wires, old sheds
Of whitewashed galvanized iron bake in the moon,
And Maurice's cats sidle in the wind.

'Gypsum takes away harshness . . . clarify
With albumen. . . .' Love failed and has become
A vineyard, carbon dioxide in dark vats
Which prickles when you thrust your arm in wine.

But through the vineyards a ghost woman walks,
Whose failure honed his art, sharpened that nose,
That long thin delicate nose which peers and sniffs
Into a long-necked glass, then passes on.

The moonlit water-tank gobbles, rumbling briefly.
A possum thumps upon the roof but Maurice
In hock-pale light is sitting at a desk
Writing in vine-scrawl of the wine he loves,

Myopic eyes given a quizzical look
By thick-lensed, rimless, gold-framed spectacles,
And always ready for a laugh, whisking
Up culinary marvels on a kerosene stove,

And once a bandicoot cooked in red wine
Greeted by ignorant cries of 'Bravo Maurice!
A champion dish!' as bits of bandicoot
Exquisitely dissolved in portly stomachs.

'I do not like machines. We use the hand-press. . . .'
Men grunt and push a handle slowly turning
Upon a metal thread, and the great press
Squeezes the grapes till Maurice calls, 'Enough!'

Feeling inside his chest (which cancer eats
Like secret phylloxera through his body)
The texture, substance, weight of grapes, that moment
The first juice breaks and floods — and it's just right.

But wine is more than art, or the fine mind
Sniffing at mathematical purities,
Or testing acidity levels in a lab;
Wine is a man inside a darkened cask,

Hunched in that primal gloom, scouring out filth,
The terror as he crawls in through the bung-hole,
Or when they haul him by his helpless arms
From that claustrophobic hole back to the world.

Wine is an ancient Catholic God, whose sun
Beats on Pokolbin earth, demanding faith,
And also works, the hand, weary from turning
The soil and dropping grapes in metal buckets.

And wine is also wisdom, which announces
As Maurice does, we should drink common wine
As well, for too much fine wine spoils the palate.
And he is quiet and shy behind his fame.

In khaki shirt and shorts, with battered hat
Maurice at vintage time stumps through his vineyard,
Dust on his forehead, sweat beneath his arms,
Retires inside the whitewashed galvanized shack

And sits and smokes, drinking a cup of coffee
Poured from an elegant metal percolator,
A taste rare then, but student days in France
And his French mother gave him a Gallic flair.

He smokes. Ah yes! But don't smoke near the cellars!
He'll cut your arm off if you smoke near there!
Those purple bubbles, maroon foam must breathe only
From polished concrete vats, cool stone, good oak.

Now Maurice sits tonight alone and humble
In summer's heart and gets up from his desk,
And pours some red, savouring it like a baby.
Night and wine, his face wavering on the glass.

Colosseum

They did not wait for this, the crowds:
Two men with a wheelbarrow in the dusk
Collecting the mess.
The muscles of a lion not quite dead
Contract as if shuddering in sleep.
The last life stops on a gently inserted knife.
Patiently, courteously the two workmen
Lift each body into the barrow
And wheel it away.
They rake the gore into the sand
And talk in undertones,
Not of Europe's vanished fauna,
The mountains which have no lions,
Birds twittering in grass amongst the empty lairs,
Africa ransacked for elephants.
They do not talk of this,
But of women and the high price of food.
And they dump the bodies
In the foul, rancid pits in the foundations,
So foul that workmen digging two thousand years later
Sickened by the smell will lay down their spades.

Plants die cleanly
In stationary impersonal conflicts
For light and water.
But the death of animals appals.
They grow legs to run from death
And death as quickly grows legs to hunt them down.
The manure of grass eaters is mild,
But the shit of man and the carnivores is corrupt,
For what they eat resents being eaten,
And when man and the animals die
The stench of the carcass
Is our last silent protest at death.

But they are not talking of this,
No, certainly not of this, our two workmen
As they come out from their underworld
Of monstrous corpses decaying in half-light.
Perhaps they wish that the pleasure seekers
Should have to go down there with them,
The frivolous children of serious fathers,
Gaudy with expensive gold and more expensive silks,
Women admiring themselves in metal mirrors,
Eating sweetmeats amongst cushions on stone tiers,
While death-yells drown in the roar of the crowd
And the florid music of hydraulic organs.

But now in the dusk as the last blood is soaked up,
There is even a kind of peace here
With the lonely rumble of an iron wheel
Across the empty arena.

from **Ross's poems**

20

A vertical line through the roof
of our house would intersect

with stars somewhere in space.
(There are other Spring Forests in the sky
and children crying. The stars
are a million mirrors of the earth.)
Closer to home this line
might bisect the moon's molten core,
and pass through stellar dust
and radiation belts,
the ozone filtering out the ultraviolet,
a tawny frogmouth flying
with a moth in its beak,
frost on our galvanized roof,
a kerosene pressure lamp perched on a book,
various texts on animal husbandry,
some short stories
and a cherrywood pipe
I have lost for years and not yet found
(That's wishful thinking—
I probably lost it in some paddock
where my eyes will never gaze down)
down through the bottom of the bookcase,
the pine floorboards,
a ginger-and-black guinea-pig asleep
beneath the house
and into red Koorawatha earth,
earth with only one need—
water for the green life chains.

If I tired of vertical lines.
I could draw a horizontal line
through this fire of ironbark logs
(with its two sounds—
the billowing and beating
of rushing blue-red air,
and the dry cindering and splitting
of timber),
a line extending through the curl

of steam from the iron kettle
warming on the flagstones,
through my moleskin trousers
as I sit on an old car seat from the Morris
(my favourite low-level armchair)
just missing Olive's legs
busily gathering tea-things,
on through the open door
of the bedroom with its black piano
carved with flowers and mandolins
(how the steel strings and sounding board
wince in our draconian ranges of temperature—
the felt hammers decayed
when my wife the musician
married me and a farm),
through the wooden walls
and a stand of red geraniums,
on past the trunk of a giant dead wattle
(I don't remove old friends,
as birds like to perch in bare branches),
and through the chicken-wire enclosure
I keep around the house and garden,
past some dogs and a fruiting fig tree,
past the cough of a fox.
I jump up with a gun and that's where that line ends.
But it's no use. Try shooting ghosts.
I come back inside.

Drinking a cup of cocoa
I draw a circle around the house
starting with the metal windmill
and creek where the ducks paddle,
but that's too wide,
I'll start my circle in closer
amongst some grass. It collects a hen
in a crater of dust, continues
through the bee-boxes with their new white paint,

on past my antique steamroller
'the slumbering giant'
and then I fetch up against that fox again
(or is it my mind?).

We have cosmic rays and cow manure,
flowers and a rusting drycleaners' van,
but there's no line around here
that will intersect a decent toilet or bathroom.

Through the dimensions I do not understand
I move
a column of living water.

38

People no longer believe what poets
or ministers of religion tell them
unless their senses say it's right.

All those cancelled Utopias,
and syllogisms that just didn't work—
relieved of the incubus of trying to believe,
I walk down my father's mountainside
one night in July, unprotected—
nothing between me and the wind
blowing from Antarctica,
nothing between me and the stars
glimmering at the bottom of space
(the Antarctica of the sky).

The wattles and native pines seem to enjoy
this cold wash of air,
this lack of illusion.
(I do not say disillusion.)

In every large city
there are a hundred or so amateur astronomers
picking their way through the sky.
I'm not that sort of fanatic.
For years if I looked through my antique brass telescope
all I could see was a broken lens
and cobwebs.

Now it's restored
I can train it by day on my father's hill
and see someone hanging out washing
up there, five miles away. . . .
Amongst tussocks and small blue daisies
invisible in the dark,
I can see the moon as large as a plate
and the rings of Saturn.

Dabbling amongst solar systems,
I'm as happy as a cow in fresh grass
with no knowledge of botany.
It's time to eat, Olive tells me.
Yes, Olive, I'm coming in
with the moon as my dinner plate.

Epithalamium

from **Nero's poems**

I

Double divorce, double disgrace
the matrons mutter. *My* Poppaea,
one glance of sunlight from your face

leaves them for dead. When we undress
stepping out from our clothes we blow
no lights out on our nakedness.

Your gaze meets mine, frank, indiscreet,
(my wife, your husband in the shadows)
hand touches buttock, our lips meet.

We hurt to love, life devours life.
Your nipple hardens touched by tongue.
Hymen's ring makes adultress wife.

II

We exchange passionate billets doux,
wild gifts if we're apart. 'Nero,
this cat . . .' 'Poppaea, goose-eggs for you . . .'

After a fight or chariot race,
my head dissolving in your lap
I lie and gaze up at your face.

In crowds you subtly lean, hands twine . . .
Some nights your lust is fierce and sudden.
Rotten with wine, your thighs ride mine.

Each glance, each kiss is contraband.
'Fancy it's you again,' we laugh
and every night's a one-night-stand.

III

Divorce, abortion — anarchy!
the stoics mutter. But the young
see dancing bodies who are free.

A million different skins — there's joy
displayed in every public baths;
beauty steams from each girl and boy.

Our bodies teach us what is true—
this bowl of cyclamens, this bed
prepared for love (as we undo

our clothes), not theories, are what's real.
I bite your arching back and breasts.
We touch and know how gods must feel.

IV

Roma, Amor reversed. The heart
of empire is our happy bed.
Rome splits when we're one hour apart.

Our rule is love. With naked skin
and naked minds we lie. I touch
your crevices, you take me in.

We screw until we're bruised and red.
Darling we're nuts. We wish to die,
we say, together in one bed.

Still moist with love, love on each face,
your cold hand clenched around my prick,
the pyre shall burn our last embrace.

The wandering tattler

I

Faint as a watermark
on the pale wash of landscape
until he separates from granite

grey encyclopaedist
of climates, piping
through the thin reed of his beak

of indecision—
the wandering tattler—
ditherer amongst geographies.

II

Eye the colour of whiskey
piping thinly
as autumn coldly laps
the stones, the wandering tattler
spreads its wings.

III

Black clouds that scarcely move,
a sandbar
midwinter
but where's the wandering tattler?

IV

A lighthouse keeper
played Mozart on a piano,
the wandering tattler
hatched eggs in dry grass.

V

The lighthouse keeper's children
write long letters;
running through the grass,
the wandering tattler
rose up before them.

VI

With his beak
jabbing a hemline in the sand—
if he's frightened,
can freeze into rock
or dead leaves.

VII

The correct temperature
is always
a migration away.
Summer in a bay
of grey rocks and marram grass
isn't exact enough,
tasting with his beak
the equations of worms
snatched from sand-slush.

VIII

Why doesn't he fly
into his mind?

IX

He pipes fluently the patois
of log cabins and seal trappers—
but who's this interloper
stitching
by the Gulf of Mexico?

X

Cryptic plumage,
weathered wood or exposed rock,
but his meaning is easy
as red berries clambering
in stubble,
belongs to no colour,
mottled,
undecided to the end.

XI

Short of breath
an old man fumbles
with the latch of a gate.
Sand dunes are covering

his fences.
At the end of a season
about to die a bird
faces cold
such as it's never known—
or heat,
it's a matter of accident.

from **Roses**

I

At night, circling weightless, we dreamed of roses,
But woke to shrapnel whining over the tundra,
Faces drained in the time of immense bombardments,
Staggering through gas and mud, eating from tins.

Clutching the crumbling edge of nothing, our minds
Reached for the tiny bursting and popping of space.
Then the guns fell silent, men climbed from their holes,
We laboured back along the roads of pain

To our first house and garden of the world,
Veterans of all denominations, lame
And agile, the convoys thundering back at sunset
To a place of weeds, cattle munching wild peaches.

The hybrid roses we had bred were gone
To briar, and all the simple climbing roses
Had rampaged high as houses thick with scent.
Iron pots were hanging in an open fireplace.

In a house of fading brick on dusty floorboards
We dreamed about a ladder to a treehouse,
Girls in silk shawls, dressed in their mothers' clothes,
A marble dropped in the grass, pears drying in trays.

By our heads an old ghost stood in calico trousers,
A mattock damp with earth glittered in his hands.
'The windlass by the well needs a new rope.
This is the childhood house you never left.'

III

In an empty house we sleep by a wicker chair.
Our boots are mudcaked, mattresses are musty.
The hives murmur all night, dark fluid in the moon.
Acres of rosebeds scent the night, roots moving

Across a path, across a mountain range,
Impulsive plants growing with jerks and pauses,
In spring the new shoots almost visibly move,
Long stems of pink wax rising from old wood.

Stepping through broken windows into fields
We find beside a spring bubbling from ironstone
A jug upon an old white-painted table.
Pink and grey parrots fly up from the pines.

IV

Watching the sky for death, starved by anger
There comes a time the soldier leaves the fields
Of agony, burned rubber, sheered-off hillsides,
A time when even hatred of injustice

Must end, when we must pardon viciousness,
Before its poison can distort the mind.
Finding the wars are infinite, the soldier
Must punch the mirror, walk through broken glass,

Wash out his blood-stained garments and discard
The crutch of hatred, walk not judging
Into a landscape scoured of noise and movement,
Only amongst some distant carob trees

In limestone hills, an old man, sunburned, digging
Is turning over dull earth, hardly noticed.
And near the trees with hanging pods are flowers,
The Changing Rose with its five petals dancing,

Ripening from yellow to buff-rose and crimson,
A butterfly amongst the ears of grass,
And Rosa Mundi's pink flesh striped with carmine,
Veined as our lives, turning upon its stem,

And in this aimless landscape is a house,
House of no argument, of sun-dried bricks,
No doors or furniture, the traveller watching
His clothes drying on a rock, birds in a bush.

V

There is no absolute rose, there are the names
And differences, the roses of a night.
The Musk, the Green Rose and the delicate Mosses,
Where do these strangers come from with their gifts?

Tangled in snow, the names, the families.
No mind or system can contain the rose.
A rose in a glass of water waits by a bed.
A child with a pencil draws a singing bird.

GEOFF PAGE (b. 1940)

Geoff Page grew up on a property near Grafton, part of a family with rural and political traditions. He was educated at the University of New England at Armidale and is now a high school teacher in Canberra. Page is a much underrated poet whose work has been inadequately represented in recent anthologies. Part of the problem is that he has only fairly recently begun to publish in sustained quantity. In the last few years it should have been recognised that he has produced a considerable amount of very individual and varied work. The language and voice of his poetry are dry and low-key, but he does create a great cumulative sense of his own world.

He is principally concerned with wastage; lost potential, lost opportunity are the basic themes of his work. There is a consistent decency and understatement and an imaginative range of sympathies throughout Page's work, which is most impressive in its totality. Having mastered the stringencies of William Carlos Williams's language, he has more recently gone on to include within his range a carefully modified version of Les Murray's high style.

In the way an earlier generation of Australian poets, such as Slessor and Webb, was concerned with the European exploration of Australia, a number of recent poets have written about Australia in the First World War; Page, with Murray and McDonald, is prominent among these.

Bondi afternoon 1915

Elioth Gruner

The wind plays through
the painted weather.

No cloud. The sea
and air, one blue.

A hemisphere
away from gunfire

an artist finds
his image for the year:

a girl in white
blown muslin, walking

in the last
clear afternoon.

Inscription at Villers-Bretonneux

The dead at Villers-Bretonneux
rise gently on a slope towards
the sky. The land is trim—skylines

of ploughed earth and steeples; unfallen
rain still hanging in the air;
confusion smoothed away

and everything put back—the village
too (red brick/white sills) in nineteen
twenty, unchanged since. Headstones

speak a dry consensus. Just one
breaks free: 'Lives Lost, Hearts Broken—
And For What?'. I think of the woman

and those she saddened by insisting—
the Melbourne clerk
who must have let it through.

Grit

A doxology

I praise the country women
of my mother's generation
who bred, brought up and boasted
six Australians each—
the nearest doctor fifty miles
on a road cut off by flood;
the women who by wordless men
were courted away from typewriters
and taught themselves to drive—
I praise their style
in the gravel corners.
I praise the snakes they broke in two
and the switch of wire they kept in a cupboard.
I praise what they keep and what they lose—
the long road in to the abattoirs,
the stare which cures
a stockman of shooting swans.
I praise the prints, the wide straw brims
they wore out to the clothes line;
I praise each oily crow that watched them.
I praise the tilting weather—
the dry creeks and the steady floods
and the few good weeks between.
I praise each column in the ledger
they kept up late by mosquito and lamp-light;
the temerity of the banker
reining them in at last—or trying;
the machinations for chequered paddocks
swung on the children's names;
the companies just one step ahead;
the tax clerk, in his way, also.
I praise each one of their six children
discovering in turn

the river in its tempers
the rapids and the river trees;
the children who grew up to horse sweat
and those who made it to the city.
I praise the stringy maxims
that served instead of prayers;
also the day that each child found
a slogan not enough,
surprising themselves in a camera flash
and bringing no extra paddocks.
I praise the boast of country women:
they could have been a wife
to any of a dozen men
and damn well made it work.
I praise what I have seen
to be much more than this.
I praise their politics of leather;
the ideologies in a line of cattle;
the minds that would not
stoop to whisky.
I praise their scorn
for the city of options, the scholars
in their turning chairs and air-conditioned theories.
I praise also that moment
when they headed off in tears—
the car in a toolshed failing to start,
a bootfull of fencing wire.
I praise the forty years
when they did not. I praise
each day and evening of their lives—
that hard abundance year by year
mapped in a single word.

Grand remonstrance

So much she never
could abide

so much always
to resent

the sulkiness
of mother's teats

the boy next door
astride her scooter

a teacher's random
sudden justice

the tardy flowering
of her breasts

the unfair cycles
of the moon

the owlish eye
of Mr Sims

over her shoulder
as she typed

the gossip that stopped
as she drew near it

the vague delays
of a fiance

leaning on
the town's opinion

the wedding with relatives
thrice-removed

the uninvited
winsome babies

the hardwon 13
carat ring

the three-day honey-
moon and then

suddenly
her own two children

the martyrdom
of 3 a.m.

the thoughtless toys
and dirty curtains

smears across
the morning light

the silences
that each child kept

seeking to
outlast her own

the son who sideslipped
out of school

the daughter year
by year resuming

her mother's skin
the husband too

his daily leavepass
to the world

the false compliance
of his slippers

and then the last
two years in bed

unvisited
and fingering

the soiled card-index
in her head

of grievance going
decades back

to taunts and snubs
in corridors

snideness in
the vivid playground

and so to a slab
of immaculate granite

the lengthening rancour
of the grave

six feet down
and now at last

the stunning
equity of death.

Prowlers

Under the thinnest
of autumn moons
they glide between houses

and vault over fences,
the night air keen
in their nostrils.

Like insects to
the lighted glass
they hover for the

classic view,
a grunting thrust
or thankful cry—

though the mute lines
of a midnight reader
will hold them just as well.

A sudden yelp
will send them
three blocks at a time;

they bark their shins
on tricycles and swear.
Sometimes

a knob will give.
They step into
the breathing rooms,

so quiet a child might ask them
dreamily for water.
Kitchen knives lie flat in drawers.

A floorboard sprung
will bring a groan
vaguely down the hall.

Angles of furniture
hold them strangely.
Books along a shelf give out

their varying degrees of light
as, guiltless yet,
they slip away—

the door pulled slowly to
across the pulse.
At half past four

they're headed homewards,
each dark house
now edged with light

and holding tight
its complement of lives.
The visitants once more

have stepped inside their own—
amazed.
Beside those heavy-

sleeping wives
two hours yet to go
until . . .

small voices
and
the morning razor.

Country drums

The drum kit dreams in a tool shed, scattered among paint tins, garden sprays and the wreckage of an old piano. Flaccid skins and snapped connections—split sticks and tangled brushes in a suitcase.

It dreams of hot burnt eucalyptus air, high above a river in the grandiose shell of a homestead, in the peak of summer, blasting out solos a hundred yards high—the river cool, duckgliding its pools below.

It dreams a jazz band wrapped around it, blowing at The Grand; raw sound jumping back from roofing iron and concrete, children pirouetting with old shearers, a fine softshoe, radio horses dashing through breaks, payment borne head high in huge cold jugs of beer.

It dreams back nights in 'lean clean hungry' country, the smell of greasy wool, 'Caravan' pounded to spidery rafters, filling the great cave of rippled iron: feeling it, too, in quieter moments, round the other way—the shed like paper, the moon high over the plateau cruising above dead trees, the cold slicked grass and scattered homesteads, one light burning.

It dreams the smalltown golf clubs, two quick rooms in fibro—one closed tight with bandits and the flow of wages, the other for dancing—Chuck Berry in the bush, the hit parade of '55 seized by immortality, a primal offbeat swinging the hips of blondes, 18, already on the edge of marriage and young men grieving wordlessly the passing of Brylcreem.

It dreams of country weddings, old Miss Keech on piano, the barber on alto sax running the evergreens with yearning vibrato, the left stick kicking up under the beat, lifting feet

still stiff from cutting burrs and fuelling coppers. It dreams
the younger sons at a bar of trestle and board drinking
towards rolled utes at 3 a.m., the odd girls sitting out
waiting a fate of five fast kids and lonely weatherboard.

It dreams back a dance in the School of Arts, the coming
and going from cars outside, the pub two miles up the road,
the blade-faced axeman with the button accordion, Mrs
McPherson of the P and C getting her say on piano, skating
kids on wax-new sawdust, a memory whiff of Irish jig, the
whole place jumping (a fruit box on stilts) and the dark
night eyes of Jerseys from a neighbouring rise of paspalum.

The drum kit dreams in a tool shed, dreams of being borne
in piece by piece through doors and grandly reassembled,
dreams taut new skins, fine wands of hickory, tall pianos,
the expectant tuning of instruments.

Cassandra paddocks

He was a reader, the great-niece says
waving a hand over tea and scones
cancelling a dozen outer paddocks
and bringing out like heirloom silver
components of a life between the lines:
the delicate mother who insisted
on Oxford for the eldest—and lost
the rest before the age of two;
the classical Tripos—the governess
began it . . . a smattering of myth,
nothing much else on these upper reaches,
curlyhaired gods the only suitors
and a classical slant to the gums.
After the young sea voyage, quiet towers,
leather shelves and well-honed conversation

he rode the paddocks differently
and left things to a string of overseers.
Stockmen held back from the distance
in his eyes, different, even deeper, than their own.
Named the paddocks Cassandra, Agamemnon,
the great-niece recalls with a laugh;
made all the wrong decisions—
instead of cattle, sheep (which went
to tallow and would not wait for wool).
But books were different.
Had them sent by the crate-load,
clipper, coastal steamer, a final
team of bullocks; the ritual
delving from straw; then open to the nose,
inhaling—a draught of laudanum.
As cedar shelves filled tight
a rim of paddocks fell to neighbours;
the perimeter tightened on the homestead
where slewing gutters and flaky paint
waited a better season.
Wresting himself from leathered air
he'd sometimes take a horse, ruminate
sales, inspect diminishing outposts,
peopling as he rode, fern gullies
with dryads and bacchantes, hearing
in a sudden rush of hooves the flight
of centaurs and in the whipbird's call
the opening note of Pan.
Ambling beside a swayback fence
he'd dream instead down his agent's list—
one book implied at least another two.
Odd trips down to Sydney to the Club
brought in the usual disappointments—
the climate, it seemed, engendered only
saleyard talk and backroom manoeuvre in railways.
Could've lost the lot, you know,
only he died first. His descendant takes

more from the uncle, riding up
after the telegram to set things straight
and hold the borders, the man who stalks
through an absence of maids
to the only real room in the house
and stops, unsettled by something
he'd never wish words to,
a wavering—in the lotus scent of leather,
before the old imperatives
could break in again to save him.

Detail

She waits at the window.
A light breeze &
a traffic smear.

From the view he had
when he was 8
& trains blew clouds

his grandmother (92)
is watching also
the railway yard.

The sill traps
a shudder of diesel—
the house is now a Home.

He comes
somehow to thank her
for white streets

of a childhood.
She looks from the window;
speaks just once . . .

of the woman
beached
in the bed behind her

both legs
cut off at the thigh.
He looks around.

Two red coals
in a crumpled face
insist

that legs till stride
from kitchen to copper
& spread each year

for children.
The silence comes again.
Grandmother & grandson.

The years are
turning transparent.
The window frames

a last half-hour,
the unbreakable logic
of trains.

ANDREW TAYLOR (b. 1940)

Now living in Adelaide as an English academic, Andrew Taylor is a graduate of Melbourne University. Some of his earlier poems are written in the style of the Melbourne academic establishment; others are more relaxed and deliberately playful. The poems here are representative of this latter approach. They both have imaginative insight, wit and stylish ease.

In more recent work, such as that collected in *The Invention of Fire,* he has adopted an Americanised, decorative form of surrealism. The attractive, personal voice of certain early poems has become heavily confessional in some of these later poems. Throughout all his stylistic shifts, though, his work can be seen to have maintained affinities with such a representative Melbourne poet as Chris Wallace Crabbe.

Slide night

1

Examine my window carefully:
it is covered with grass—thrown up
by the mower and stuck because it was
even at 3.30 yesterday
still wet with dew. It's going brown.
Some insect has laid twelve rows
of eggs, fragment of a giant
thumbprint—nature's—in a corner.
It's dirty, and paint spatters it
from a bad paint job. Moths crawling.

2

Put it under the microscope.
Do you see the man, head full
of grass, moth eggs, paint,
sitting at a desk? See insects
clamber through his eyes, ferret his ears
for light, twaddle his page?
Stamped in one corner, Certified
Fit To Rage? A host of caterpillars
populate and perish out of that script?

3

Or flash it on a screen (memories
of the Uffizzi and/or was it Utrecht?)
a meadow scholar, flowery page be-sprent,
or a firm burgher, pastoralised.
In one corner the museum stamp,
inscrutable as a postmark from Taiwan.

4

From here, inside, it's largely black
—because it's night—and that's where you are,
all of you: in the dark! Moths,
heads ablaze, patrol my image
my giant ghost on the glass,
merino bodies quiver at my eye.
Larger than the huntsman I am the sky.
My galloping fingers sweep the universe. No stars.
Moths instead, heads flaming as Betelgeuse.

5

Switch out the show. It's time to sleep. To sleep.
My head expands to the brilliance of a quasar,
space swallows my wavelength, hour after hour.

The nocturne in the corner phonebox

Someone is playing a trombone
in the telephone box outside my room.
It's 1 a.m.,
and he's removed the globe.
He's playing a melancholy cadenza
probably over the S.T.D.
to his girl in Sydney.

I can imagine . . .
she's curled to the telephone
listening to that impossible music
a smile curving her face.
I wonder if he has enough change
for all those extensions.
Could he reverse the charge?

Somebody called Hugh Adamson
blares out a nocturne in a phone box.
His father's old and dying,
his mother's dead, his girl's away,
he's very sad, his nocturne's very sad,
his trombone blares and flares and says
'He's very sad, yair yair, he's very sad'.

Maybe he's only playing to a friend
in East St. Kilda.
Maybe he hasn't any change.
Someone is playing a trombone—impossible—
in the phone box with the door shut.
I've no idea who he is. I'm waiting
for my phone to ring. I like this music.

ALLEN AFTERMAN (b. 1940)

Having graduated in law at Harvard, Allen Afterman came to Australia and taught company law in Melbourne. After he started publishing poetry he settled on an isolated farm on the south coast of New South Wales.

There is in his work an acute horror of human suffering and cruelty. His poems dealing with the Holocaust are outstanding. He has also written poems about farm life, which show a desire to regain an Edenic relationship with the land. These poems are direct and explicit, like all his work, but lack the power of the poems about Jewish suffering. His writing is severe, bare and conveys his voice with rhythmical exactitude. The poems selected here have a sense of passionate personal involvement which is unusual amongst current poets.

The real is not enough

> *The real is not enough: through*
> *its disguise*
> *Tell us the truth*
> *which fills the mind with light.*
>> Jozsef Attila.

No one
is here.
Not even at the gate.

Squinting, I keep going
mind reeling . . .
Liebe Mutter! if my eyes had seen these buildings,
if they had seen this place *then*.

As far as the eye can see
fences, towers, barracks

in glare.
Hot grey haze
vast—
hopeless—

my head lowers.

* * *

A narrow mud path
mown from one barrack
to the next—

I walk up
down

Hour
upon hour

. . . the women's section
the families' section
the gipsies' section
floating in weeds.

Trains hoot, shunt:

a railroad track leads straight
to a mass of rubble.

I look for blood droplets,
scratch marks.

* * *

. . . Somewhere
a group is laughing, they are shouting a girl's name—

A family passes, they read
a guide-book out loud, like a lecture—

Every word carries like a shot—

I want to scream: are you *crazy?*

I rip out a handful of flowering weeds.

. . . anyhow,
I've seen enough.
I won't be the keeper of this place.

The teenagers scramble up into a guard tower—

Someone loudly translates the crematorium sign—

I break a strand of rusted barbed wire,
hide it in my sleeve.
In my pocket, dried rotten straw
from a bunk in the women's section.

Others are coming, a group is leaving their bus . . .

I walk out
with no thoughts, feet burning

along the desolate main camp road—

What is the truth which fills the mind with light?

Birkenau, 1977

The ceremony for Mr Najdek

A certain Pole,
a short, bespectacled bureaucrat,
once a friend of Meir

flown into Jerusalem,
now stands at attention
. . . the cantor is singing, the rabbi prays,
the administrators speak in his honour.

From Borislav he supported a world:
night and day he refused to be dishonoured—
two years he lived beyond human nature.
Day by day
in his attic

in caves

in drains
he saved the Meirs.
            . . . he fills the hole with vigour.

                              Rising,
he says something in Polish which attracts laughter; then,
L'Chai'm!

As the group leaves the Memorial Room
        I break through
                    trying to touch his arm—

                                        Jerusalem, 1976

L'Chai'm: To life!

Morning   noon   and night

Months pass, Hungary pumps like an artery
judenfrei.
Eden has put the proposal to the Secretary of Air:
the Jews are being deported, the Nazis defeated,
in retreat (this is 1944)—
when will they bomb the camps and its railways?
Each week the B.B.C. broadcasts atrocities,
a half-million lives are at stake.

Months pass . . .
the wretches look to the sky each night:
the commandants plan their escape—
intelligence flows in—timetables,
targets, detailed plans (pilots volunteer)

each morning   noon   and night
in a frenzy of a last meal, the ovens are gorged.

One prayer drifts over the camps—

   Stalin   Churchill   Roosevelt

ROGER McDONALD (b. 1941)

Son of a Presbyterian minister, McDonald spent his childhood in
country towns, and is a graduate of Sydney University. He has worked
for the ABC as a producer of feature programmes, and was poetry editor

for the University of Queensland Press when it published its innovative and wide-ranging series of Paperback Poets. Since then, and since publishing two volumes of his own poetry, McDonald has become a successful novelist, and has settled on a farm near Canberra with his wife, Rhyll McMaster, and family.

All but the last of the poems used here are from *Airship*, McDonald's second book and one of the most remarkable single collections of recent years. These poems are highly individual: while not formalistic, they often have an alien, mechanistic precision and sheen to them. They sometimes seem analogous to the Metaphysical art of the painter De Chirico. The natural objects and machines which McDonald presents have a hostile energy of their own, and human control is always fragile. His recurring theme is insecurity. The originality of certain of his poems may owe something to science-fiction writers.

Bachelor farmer

At half-past five—the earth cooling,
the sweat of his shirt
soaked up in red dirt—
he tunnels his arm through the weight
of a bag of wheat, slowly withdraws it,
and sees how the yellow grains
shiver, as though magnetized away
from his skin, each one alone and trembling.

Walking beside the fence, in another paddock,
he discovers a grain
caught in the hairs of his wrist;
he bends down, allows it to fall,
and with the careful toe of his boot
presses it into the ground.

All night sprawled on the verandah of his hut,
he wakes to the call of the pallid cuckoo,
its blunted scale
low on the heads of unharvested wheat—

not rising towards him, not falling away,
but close by, unchanging, incomplete.

Sickle beach

Sickle beach,
bay like a wine glass.
Butterflies launch themselves
eastward from marram grass.

Lemon, the lower sky,
apricot air.
Who would believe a man
died close to here?

Came, on a blue day,
easy, on horseback.
Slipped, and broke his head
hard on a rock.

Blood in the rippled light,
a word of surprise:
Me? It is not true.
Thus a man dies.

Thus, in the empty hills,
blackberries increase,
rabbits and wild cats
run through the house.

Two summers in Moravia

That soldier with a machinegun bolted
to his motorcycle, I was going to say
ambled down to the pond to take
what geese he wanted; but he didn't.

This was whole days before the horizon trembled.

In the farmyard all the soldier did
was ask for eggs and milk.
He and the daughter (mother sweeping)
stood silent, the sky rounded
like a blue dish.

This was a day
when little happened,
though inch by inch everything changed.
A load of hay narrowly crossed the bridge,
the boy caught a fish underneath in shade,
and ducks quarreled in the reeds.
Surrounded by wheat, everyone heard the wind
whisper, at evening, as though grain already threshed
was poured from hand to hand.

This was a day possible to locate, years later,
on a similar occasion; geese alive,
the sky uncracked like a new dish,
even the wheat hissing with rumour.
I was going to say unchanged
completely, but somewhere behind
the soldier had tugged his cap,
kicked the motor to harsh life
and swayed off,
the nose of the machinegun tilted up.

Precise invaders

Backs in whipping broom,
high-stepping up a path of wind
that lifts from darkness in the valley floor—
unexpected, and quick, their rumps
like turned-down lanterns at a secret run—
three deer, wheeling left through broken stone
and crossing cattle grass to leap
as if to balance there
against a wall of pines, in smoky light,
alert for admiration: bounding the wire
in rapt succession, with such perfect flight
they leap inside my dreams of how they leapt.

The enemy

The enemy conspires to end
heartbeat, grass growth, clouds
and the life of the wind.
He wishes to extinguish
among all things
the life of the sun.

In the present campaign
his weapons are notions of spring.
See where he pauses, an insidious flower
propped on the roots of a tree.
Modest, deceitful, infiltrating.

The enemy's careful advance
halts at rocks and the sea.
An alliance is formed, although
these also
he marks for mortality.

Incident in Transylvania

Black in a tentlike cloak, at rest
near the roots of an ancient oak on a hillside
the Count awaits a two-legged bottle.

Soon, awkward astride a mule, plunking with lurches
his winded guitar, a corpuscular friar
with lymphocytes fizzing like spa water
rides through a curtain of sweat
till his chin clicks up
on the outstretched arm of the Count who is waiting.

A surprise, like cactus clapped to his neck:

'I've been watching your ride,' lips the Count,
with ruby politeness. The friar has bubbles
of breakfast loose in his throat,
and riffles a pack of escapes:
'I'mer, willyar, issalltoo . . . too . . .' and slumps
to the pit of his belly, waiting.

But the Count draws back from capture, strangely,
and it isn't the friar's fat, or the odour of fear
that deters him, nor even a whiff of chubby religion.
There are personal bones that give trouble—
nights of competing with shadows,
the knuckle and knee-bruising hunts,
the general ascent in the land
of inferior blood.
'It's a pain in the fangs,' he snaps,
heeling the mule in the butt,
bouncing the friar in whistles downhill.

Back at the castle the groom has observed that the Count
seems no longer himself, no longer deliciously flensed

by the howl of his creatures (those slack
acres of flesh in cylindrical pits)
no longer—the servants gather and mutter—
no longer the Count of the cloak and the eye, the limp,
and the dreaded formula.

He calls for a glass of milk, he calls
for news of the world and a hot brown bun,
while a little old wife appears in the room's far corner,
clucking and knitting, nursing a cat,
blinking her blue old eyes and snicking her lips for a chat.

The hollow thesaurus

Names for everything I touch
were hatched in bibles, in poems cupped by madmen
on rocky hills, by marks on sheets of stone,
by humped and sticky lines in printed books.
Lexicographers burned their stringy eyeballs black
for the sake of my knowing. Instinctive generations
hammered their victories, threaded a chain,
and lowered their strung-up wisdom in a twist
of molecules. But with me in mind
their time was wasted.

When the bloodred, pewter, sickle, sick or meloned moon
swells from nowhere,
the chatter of vast informative print
spills varied as milk. Nothing prepares me
even for common arrivals like this.

Look. The moon comes up. Behind certain trees are bats
that wrench skyward like black sticks.
Light falls thinly on grass, from moon and open door.
This has not happened before.

Apis mellifica

In a dreamlike fall, the long
spoon in the honey-jar descends—a bubble going

down, he thinks, a silver bell.
He stands there a while,

humming, twisting the spoon
slowly from side to side. (The moon

drops from an amber-coloured cloud,
on the horizon a metal sphere rides

heavily over water, hunting the crushed ocean floor.)
Fifteen pounds of honey in the tall jar—

nectar, the fall of pollen, bees in the Yellow Box tree
filling that flowery head once a year

with a huge thought, all of it here.
Now the spoon climbs up as though something

is spoken by light
and shade in their alternating

vowels of movement, and held—as though what the tree
thought
was taken away and stored,

deepened, like an old colour, and understood.

JENNIFER RANKIN (1941-1979)

Jennifer Rankin studied at Sydney University after a childhood in the country. She was married to the painter David Rankin and died of cancer at the age of thirty-eight. Two books of her poetry appeared during her lifetime and another book remains unpublished, but a collected work is to be produced.

Her early poems are evocations of landscape and childhood; later there is an attempt to write more primitively, with something of the aboriginals' sense of the spirit of place. Death became a recurrent theme. These later poems have heavily end-stopped lines and staccato rhythms. Abandoning the mellifluous effects of her early work, the poet relies on repetition and circularity, which conveys her inability to escape her entrapment.

Cicada singing

A bird is chasing the cicada!
I see them skim over the thin grass

into the trees.

And last night cicada they nearly had you,
my skinny son and his friend,

shimmying up gumtrees in the cool dark street
coming home tired and unsuccessful.

Shall I tell them tonight
you are in that tree?

With your life expectancy
six days in the sun
eight years in the earth
and the long slow crawl behind you?

Shall I tell them tonight?

Ah! but the probing beak of the bird
prizes you out!
Quick in the swift air
it is the urgent flap of bird-wind

and you glint green my cicada
in this instant-wheeling-garden
you glint green
under the weight of the bird

you glint green and the sun shines

catching itself on your newly-dried wings
that tear like a child's first transfer in the air.

Williamstown

1

The thin brown house waits with me
while the wind roughs up the bay

before us the bulk flour containers
upright on their single railway track

stand still, while at the other side
the seasky wrestles gently with the city for a line.

2 South Willie Sunday

A container ship broke some of the sky's space
just then when it sailed by up the bay,
blocking out the city that lay behind
filling my window with irregular coloured shape

now it is gone and the waves are soothing

you would not believe in boys with chequered coats
riding their rough ponies before weekend cars
not bothering to check the sea over their shoulder
or the pane of glass where I sit.

3 South Willie Tuesday

That time it was a Spaniard on a bicycle
who rode out of the bulk flour container
frame of my window, past the Magritte backdrop
where the horses graze behind the trainline
in front of the sea, past the telegraph pole
and the slogan slapped silos into the opposite frame

where true views of seagulls must surely begin.

4 South Willie weather

Choppy seas was the forecast yesterday.
The day before the seas were smooth.
Today you turned to me and the sea did hesitate.

NICHOLAS HASLUCK (b. 1942)

A Western Australian, Nicholas Hasluck is a partner in a Perth firm of solicitors, and has published two novels and a book of short stories, as well as two collections of poetry.

His verse is distinguished by its imaginative themes, as in 'Islands', included here. While the technique is conservative, the content is often questioning and satirical. His tone is epicurean, presenting a sceptical enjoyment of the world. He proceeds by means of image and understatement. Hasluck has written a number of verse sequences, and the two extracts here from 'Rottnest Island' demonstrate his ability to achieve an effect by juxtaposing detail, while absenting himself as a personality from the poem.

Islands

Islands which have
never existed
have made their way
on to maps nonetheless.

And having done so
have held their place,
quite respectably,
sometimes for centuries.

Voyages of undiscovery, deep
into the charted wastes,
were then required
to move them off.

The Auroras, for instance.
Beneath Cape Horn.
Sighted first in 1762
and confirmed by
Captain Manuel de Oyarvido
thirty years later.

But since the voyage of
someone whose name
escapes me, on a date
I can't quite remember—
they are now known
not to exist.

Cartographers—hands high
in the frail rigging of
latitudes and longitudes—
wiped them out, reluctantly.

And so, some mariners,
who pushed beyond the pale,
forfeit the names they left
in lonely seas.

Remember them.
Respect their enterprise.
It takes a certain
kind of boldness
to have seen such
islands first of all.

In the mind's atlas,
footnotes, like broken rules,
are not without importance.

Who found America?

Those canny trawlers,
absent for months,
fishing the depths,
must have been somewhere
with their sealed lips.

from **Rottnest Island**

V

Christmas Day. 1696.
Came to the Southland.
Drew back. Approached
an island five leagues
from the main shore,
bays and rocky outcrops.
Waited four days.

Gloves for the oarsmen;
extra rations in the boats
going ashore. Arrived at
early light; glad to be
over the reef, touching land.
Anchored safely. De Vlamingh
to his own tent. Then, night.

Birds floating to our hands.
Surmounted some low hills.
A clover leaf of lakes at
the centre, mostly brine.

Walked northwards. Lizards,
reptiles. A rat-like creature
hunching its back; droppings
like loathsome birds' eggs.
Spiky bracken. Limestone.
No signs of habitation.

Returned to the ship after
three days. The Southland
hazy in the morning sun.
Set sail . . .

VI

All day the bicycles come and go
from General Store to bungalow.

From bungalow to Bakery and back
to get the makings for a midday snack.

At night, again, like carefree ships,
the bikes drift past on random trips.

Down to the Tearooms beneath the stars,
a younger brother on the handlebars.

To visit the pub; friends, perhaps.
Jokes about fishing; afternoon naps.

A hand of cards and a quiet beer.
The days cycle past, year by year.

Cycling back to the bungalow,
we can see the mainland lights aglow.

Out there, way out, that luminous shelf,
the haze of light and the city itself.

ROBERT ADAMSON (b. 1944)

Adamson's boyhood was spent mainly on the Hawkesbury River, and this landscape, and the estuarine fishing which members of his family were involved in, remain the setting for what is probably his best poetry.

In his youth, Adamson spent time in reform school and gaol, where he discovered his interest in writing. He has been editor of *New Poetry* magazine for many years, and has designed and published most of his own books as well as the work of a circle of young poets.

The influences on his work include Rimbaud and the Americans Robert Duncan and Robert Creeley. The major theme of his poetry is ambivalence, between the desire to escape guilt in a consciously romanticised merging with nature, and a rejection of guilt and social restrictions through the assertion of self.

My house

My mother lives in a house
where nobody has ever died

she surrounds herself
and her family with light

each time I go home
I feel she is washing
and ironing the clothes of death

these clothes for work
and for going out
to the Club on Sunday
and for Jenny to take her baby
to the doctor in

death comes on the television
and mum laughs

saying there's death again
I must get those jeans taken up

The mullet run

Gone for days, and way down the river—
an old man? We sat around the 'Angler's Rest'
playing the jukebox: Slim Dusty

saving us from talk. I played with my
rum and Coke. We were home by midnight, walked
all the way to Mooney, and christ—

where was he, as if I didn't know. I slept on
the verandah to overlook a slackening tide.
3 a.m. my cousin came back to say

she loved me—soon I would explore my sensual
dream, and Lindy's beery breath—like
I'd planned all those months. A southerly,

of course, blew up just before dawn, ripping
canvas from the window frames; branches
snapped clean off the mulberry tree outside

to fall across the bed. Our calico
sheets were soaked with rain and sticky dark
stains. Almost half the rusty

corrugated iron blew from the roof,
and, really, what could've I done? Wind dropped,
dawn, sun in the slanting mulberry tree.

It was midday before our grandfather
finally got back. We heard his boat down beside
the wharf—I stayed in the house

pretending to clean up. By the time he came
through the front door, saw the roof half gone,
and said there'd been a mullet run,

we knew somehow he didn't want to know.
I couldn't have told him then, but needed him
to ask. We just followed him down

to his trawler, helping pack mullet into
boxes of crushed ice. Lindy was the first to go,
she dropped everything and ran.

I knew he didn't really want me there,
but held on for a while at any rate—and then
filled a kero tin with mullet gut,

carried it up the yard, and sat there an hour
feeding it to his chooks. The scales curling in
the sun, falling from my arms.

BRIAN DIBBLE (b. 1943)

An American by birth, now living in Western Australia and lecturing in English at the West Australian Institute of Technology, Dibble has published only a few poems in magazines. We have included this one because of its sensuality and tight formal realisation. The poem has previously appeared in Fay Zwicky's anthology, *Quarry*.

Maine

There is a skunk
musk in the air.
There is a light
snow on the ground.
The sky is dark
cold April air.
The old bathtub
is on the lawn.
I am in it
(nude, in the tub,
in hot water,
carried from the
kitchen in a
clam-steaming pot).
There are small stars,
distant lights
(on the island
across the bay).

There is a fire
in the fireplace.
My towel warms
there and a girl
(in a red robe)
waits there. I smell
the smoke, mixing
with the skunk musk.
But I am here
(up to my neck,
my head is bathed
in steam), smelling
skunk musk, fire smoke.
I stand and the
steam rises with
me (small stars
no longer clear,
distant lights
obscured). I pull
the plug and the
snow near the drain
of the tub stains.

NIGEL ROBERTS (b. 1941)

The image of Nigel Roberts in his work is that of the grand old man of
Balmain poetry (Balmain: Sydney's Haight-Ashbury); one of the first
and last exponents here of Beat poetics. Roberts is much undervalued:
he writes the funniest poetry in Australia at present, and is also a

meticulous craftsman. Under his battered, street-wise persona, there is considerable affection for people, real sexiness and vitality, poignance and self-knowledge. From New Zealand, he has lived in Australia for a couple of decades, and teaches art at a high school.

Roberts has published little, not just because he is 'too busy living', which is his explanation, but because he is exacting about his work. In support of this, see 'As Bruce Beaver does' in Tom Shapcott's anthology *Australian Poetry Now*, for its much less refined earlier version. 'The quote from Auden' is a popular poem at public readings. 'The gull's flight' and 'The house special' are more recent works. This last poem is from a group of poems written as the result of travelling in America.

The quote from Auden

1

at the conclusion of breakfast
in that space / moment / question
of the first cigarette
or the washing up
She / relayed
The Quote
from Auden.

I faked
message received & understood
thinking it
offering / or her
inductive incidental to
the day & its work
I knew only that
it was / a quote from Auden.

later
I found the book / publicly open
annotated

       & underlined in
     too true—
   in her signatory agreement
  with / the quote from Auden.

     & again / later
   in a brief drink at the pub
    'R' enthusiastically
     told 'M' & 'C'
   who looked sharply / in
     my direction
   the quote from Auden.

Some deal / there was hint
was going down
            I knew its key
in the quote from Auden.

2

   I talked of everything but
    at the Bon Gout
    to affirm fuck
     & deny
   after dinner screw—
          unsuccessfully
how could i
   in a doz words / a score
    be briefed
   to hold the floor with
   the quote from auden.

   as she showered
 i fed the animal computors
  the encoded dactyls
  broadcast on her skin
   & in their readout
   the quote from auden

& the gnostic glossolalia
of suck / oh jesus
fuck me bite
you're the best / on top
dont move—
She really meant
the quote from auden.

3

from then on   all speech
action   written word
in part or principle
deferred to
the quote from auden

on T shirts / the quote from auden
from umpire Brooks or the Hill to Michael Holding
after bowling
3 consecutive bumpers at Redpath
the quote from auden.
Joni Mitchell's next album / the quote from auden
& then at 11 / the news & weather
followed by the quote from auden
graffiti on the Annandale underpass
the quote from auden
every future kiss tainted with / the quote from auden
a most quotable / quote / the quote from auden
get the boot in first / the same applies
with the quote from auden

so   i was introduced to
her intent—
—TO QUIT
Sock it to me—
The quote from auden

I cannot
be true
to love
or it
true to me
is one interpretation
of the quote
from auden

'Come live with me & be my love
& we shall all the pleasures prove'
is not
the quote from auden

Sock it to me—
one more time.

the quote
from auden

Reward / for a missing deity

maybe / yr on sabbatical
maybe yr in the dunny / reading yr reviews
maybe yr in the Pacific / on a Women's Weekly Cruise
& maybe
yr preparing a statement for the six o'clock news
that perhaps
you were trapped in a ski hut / by an avalanche
of Betty Hutton

maybe / yr a war criminal / farming in Chile
maybe yr tapping phones / of subscribers to Dial a Prayer
maybe yr breaking that record / buried alive
12 ft underground

maybe yr weeping / in Farmer's Lost & Found
or perhaps
yr taking an angel out to lunch

maybe / yr in conference
or hitting off from the Club House tee
maybe yr demanding / a fat personal appearance fee
maybe yr on strike / & wont accept / arbitration
maybe yr being impeached / for yr crook administration
or perhaps
yr competing / in a Twist Marathon / on Taiwan

maybe / yr doing / In Service Training
maybe yr delivering newspapers
to pay yr way through Uni
maybe yr doing / Pestilence & Famine / I
& Destruction II

maybe yr on safari / collecting / for a private zoo
or perhaps
you farted / & very quickly / left the room

maybe / yr a casualty / of future shock
maybe yr in the mountains / plotting revolution
& a second coming
maybe yr the phantom of the opera / alone in the box
maybe yr wanking over Japanese woodcuts
of geishas sucking cocks
or perhaps
yr being interviewed by Frost / Fantastic / or Hef.

maybe / yr establishing an alibi
maybe yr being / held / incommunicado
maybe yr holed up / in Chicago
with a contract on yr head
maybe yr loneing it in Denver
in boxcars / boxcars boxcars

maybe you've been transfered to another branch
maybe yr in Paekakariki
maybe yr in Nimbin
maybe yr walking / nicotine desperate / up the road
& perhaps
yr going to be back in five minutes

But
& most probably
i would think—
you were horribly scarred
in a laboratory accident / &
yr too sensitive / to
show yr face.

As Bruce Beaver does

jesus—
robert graves
is in town / & giving a reading / at
the town hall / wednesday
night.

last week
terry & i / went
to speak with a friend
an established poet—
the conversation / was literary
our work
carlos williams
graves on yeats / etc
institutions / &
asylums.

HE / HAS IT / MADE—
he is settled in this business / of
the particular & universal
reality of things—
the poet at his desk / sharpening
his pencils / & checking
that the bookcase is in order.

a poet is a man / who
camphors his chest / &
inhales / the mendicant air
of himself.

The house special

Bellino
of Dynek International
has ordered
a Whiskey Sour
so, I punt
on a Banana Daiquiri
the House Special.

That's a fags drink
declares Bellino
as he moves
to checkout
a chick
with whom he's established
some eye contact

Hold the Daiquiri
Chuck
a Gin & Tonic—
& I follow

This is Nigel
from Australia
Hello,
Hi;
but I dont catch her name
as Bellino is hustling
the conversation on
from, the who are you
to the, who
she wants to be.

& she is telling him
of her spotlight ambition
to be a singer
a variant of Roberta Flack
& in time
a piano bar
or a small club
somewhere

the sometime
& somewhere schedule
sets Bellino's index
pecking at her left tit
as he believes in
Target Setting
Assertiveness, &
Self Maximization
to which
he puts his wallet on the bar
& asks her price
on ten Carnegie Hall tickets
in a years time
because, if she wants to
thats where she could be.

Well
the singer demurs
as I gofer
new drinks;
& apparently I miss something
for when I return
Bellino is stabbing at that breast
again

I told you
I dont eat
garbage
& you
are feedin me
garbage,
crap
& garbage.

Well that's the way
it goes, she says
Thanks for the advice
& drinks, but
Ive got a vocal coach
in the morning

You win some
you lose some
says Bellino
who then pays
his tab
& goes

So. Im cut loose
in the Valley Bar & Grill
just on closing
One, on the house
asks Chuck

what will it be?
& without hesitation
I say
a Banana Daiquiri

One
Banana
Daiquiri
comin up
says Chuck

The gull's flight

      The gull's flight
is low
             flat
   & hard

     they go
to sea
       to the edge
where the day's fire
       is lit

     they go
as shiftworkers
       to the dawn.

JOHN TRANTER (b. 1943)

After growing up on a farm on the south coast of New South Wales, John Tranter went to Sydney University, and has worked in publishing and broadcasting. In the early seventies he brought out a number of underground magazines, and more recently has published books of poetry by John Forbes, Susan Hampton, Rae Desmond Jones and Martin Johnston. He edited *The New Australian Poetry,* an anthology of the 'generation of '68'.

In many of his poems Tranter has adopted the role of having nothing to say, excluding all coherent subject matter, so that his writing resembles a series of deliberately unrelated movie stills. The tone is clinical, the subject often violent; many poems have a refrigerated wit. This cerebral approach is much influenced by recent New York poetry. All of his poems are well-crafted, and in some there is an acknowledged humanity and a real perceptiveness about people; we have represented this side of his work. 'At the Criterion' and 'The letter' are both recent poems.

Sonnet 47

He's older now, and has learnt the need to survive.
The evening's carefully planned, down to the wine;
his income hangs on a favour. Guests arrive,
important, cautious, not quite ready to dine,
accepting a sherry, behind the uneasy levity
catching a thread of music from another room,
politely not noticing the unobtrusive poverty,
looking to see who sits next to whom.

The conversation drifts: who's been betrayed
by the one you'd least expect; who's up, who's down,
who left for political reasons, and who stayed.
An awkward pause at the door. Not much is said.
The engine coughs, a car door slams. They're gone.
He has a terrible headache. He goes to bed.

Sonnet 55

for Reinhold Karlssen

Waiting and waiting, there's an end to it.
Eating bad food, sleeping on the floor,
there's an end to that too. One day
your enemies reach out of your head quickly
and take you to the cold and dirty places,
and you're too old for that sort of thing.
The bad music keeps you there, and makes you cruel,
and you are the loved one you are least kind to.

Waiting and waiting for the good weather,
there's a hard art in that, and a sour man—
too old for that sort of punishment—does it badly.
But one day you wake up and go back home and if you're
tough and lucky you leave most of it behind. Eating
good food, accepting kindness—there's an art in that.

At the Criterion

for Martin Johnston

I don't go to the pub much any more—
they pulled down the Newcastle ten years ago,
and the Forest Lodge is full of young punks
who can't hold their drink. But now and then—

say, some Friday night when my room
gets on my nerves, with its endless books,
with the pool of lamplight on the table,
the traffic outside my window,
the crowds, the rush and babble, then,
just for old times' sake, I go out.
And she's sure to be there, in the corner bar,
laughing with that young executive
who goes down to the snow in the winter
and has a town house in Double Bay.
They look happy enough. He seems
quite at ease and familiar with her,
though he's only known her a few months—
does he know yet, for example,
that she had an abortion two years ago,
at seventeen, and still isn't over it?
That her mother won't speak to her now
because of the 'immoral things' she did
with her pretty room-mate at College;
that she likes Seafood Avocado, and can't stand
cats, or poverty; and when she makes love
with that awkward desperation, sad and hurried—
at that peak of moaning frenzy
brief tears gather in her eyes: she's not crying,
not happy, just 'a bit out of it', as she says.
Well, he'll learn these things, if he's
attentive, and if it lasts long enough.
Even now—and I'm only on my seventh drink—
she's paying rather too much attention to that
academic type near the door—an older man,
good-looking in a rough sort of way;
a drunk, but with a charming line of talk.
And she prefers older men.
                              When I've had enough
I'll go back to the flat and pour a scotch
and read over my notes on Cavafy—
a Greek poet, dead long ago,

who lived very fast when he was young
then spent a lonely middle age remembering
his youth in Alexandria, the sordid affairs . . .
patiently sketching a portrait of his
beautiful, corrupt and much-loved city—
'its fever, its absolute devotion to pleasure.'

The letter

Susan thought that she'd forgotten
those shameful things. It must be
twenty years since that girl's body
writhed under Susan's touch,
her young body, firm and scented . . .
memories like that are better buried.
Then this aerogramme from Tucson,
littered with her awkward scrawl:
now, it seems, she's thirty-eight, wrecked
in some American kitchen,
worried about the children, overweight.
A pay packet is torn up,
tears ravage her face,
things have gone from bad to worse,
says her pathetic letter. **Susan,
write to me, I'm so unhappy.** Serve her right.
Susan pours another glass of wine
and tries to read a book, but nothing works:
the rain scribbles its misery across the window,
a heap of leaves is scattered on the lawn.
Maybe her memory lies, perhaps
the girl was plain and commonplace.
Judging from her letter, she's a fool.
There were nasty things, too:
haggling over money, other women,
horrible fights. It lasted one season,

through winter rain, and ended badly.
But her limbs, moving on the bed
in the warm glow of the lamp, her kisses,
her body bucking uncontrollably
and the way she cried out . . . ah, so long ago.
Twenty years — you can't blame her for crying:
it's raining, she's forty, she's alone.

CHRISTINE CHURCHES (b. 1945)

Christine Churches is a South Australian poet, married to an Anglican
clergyman. She has a family of four young children. Her short poems
are always distinguished by original phrasing or imagery, and often
have rural or family subject-matter. She has published only one small
pamphlet, though her work continues to appear in magazines.

My mother and the trees

She shook the doormat free of dogs,
struck the tank to measure water, as she
marshalled us with iron buckets
to carry rations for the trees.

From fibres of air, she wove
us there the hope of leaves,
and in the flat and tepid dust
she dreamed a dwelling place of shade.

Summer by summer we carted water, slopped
lopsided up and back across the paddock:
the promised land a skeleton of stakes and hessian,
her voice insistent that they lived.

Reluctant slaves and unbelievers,
we sat out of sight
with our feet in the buckets, as she
filled the sky to the brim with trees.

ROBERT GRAY (b. 1945)

Robert Gray grew up in the then small country town of Coffs Harbour,
on the north coast of New South Wales. He left school early and has
worked in Sydney, at first in advertising agencies and then mainly in
bookshops, and has done much reviewing.

His poetry is written in a variety of free shapes, ranging from a subverted formalism with rhyme and half-rhyme, through the use of a
fluctuating line length, to prose poems. D. H. Lawrence and William
Carlos Williams were early influences; also Japanese verse—he has
written many haiku. The main preoccupation of his poetry is the
relationship of man to nature. He has been attracted to Taoist and
Buddhist philosophy, and has endeavoured to locate the essentials of
these within the Western tradition, and to experience them in the
Australian environment. A number of his poems are autobiographical,
and many others are political, dealing with social underdogs or the
destruction of place. His poems are descriptively precise, and he has
taken the use of visual imagery to an extreme, making particular use,
since he is anti-symbolist, of simile. 'Poem to my father' is written in

William Carlos Williams's 'variable foot', and is atypical of his work in
its reliance on anecdote rather than imagery for its effect.

Gray is given to reworking poems after their publication in book
form, and most of those here vary from previously published versions.
Such revision is sometimes undertaken to resolve the convoluted and
expressionist syntax of his earlier poems.

The meat works

Most of them worked around the slaughtering
out the back, where concrete gutters
crawled off
heavily, and the hot, fertilizer-thick,
sticky stench of blood
sent flies mad,
but I settled for one of the lowest-paid jobs, making mince
right the furthest end from those bellowing,
sloppy yards. Outside, the pigs' fear
made them mount one another
at the last minute. I stood all day
by a shaking metal box
that had a chute in, and a spout,
snatching steaks from a bin they kept refilling
pushing them through
arm-thick corkscrews, grinding around inside it, meat or not—
chomping, bloody mouth—
using a greasy stick
shaped into a penis.
When I grabbed it the first time
it slipped, slippery as soap, out of my hand,
in the machine
that gnawed it hysterically a few moments
louder and louder, then, shuddering, stopped;
fused every light in the shop.

Too soon to sack me—
it was the first thing I'd done.
For a while, I had to lug gutted pigs
white as swedes
and with straight stick tails
to the ice rooms, hang them by the hooves
on hooks—the dripping blood was solidified
like candle-wax—or pack a long intestine
with sausage meat.
We got meat to take home—
red plastic bags with the fat showing through.
We'd wash, then
out on the blue metal
towards town; but after sticking your hands all day
in snail-sheened flesh,
you found, around the nails, there was still blood.
I didn't usually take the meat.
I'd walk home on
the shiny, white-bruising beach, in mauve light,
past the town.
The beach, with those startling, storm-cloud mountains, high
beyond the furthest fibro houses, the reason
I stayed. (The only work
was at this Works.)—My wife
carried her sandals, in the sand and beach grass,
to meet me. I'd scoop up shell-grit
and scrub my hands,
treading about
through the icy ledges of the surf
as she came along. We said that working with meat was like
burning-off the live bush
and fertilizing with rottenness,
for this frail green money.
There was a flaw to the analogy
you felt, but one
I didn't look at, then—
the way those pigs were stuck there, clinging onto each other.

To the master Dōgen Zenji
(1200-1253 A.D.)

Dōgen came in and sat on the wood platform,
all the people had gathered
like birds upon the lake.

After years, he'd come back from China,
and had brought no scriptures—he showed them
empty hands.

This was in Kyoto
at someone-else's temple. He said, All that's important
is the ordinary things.

Making the fire
to boil some bathwater, pounding rice, pulling the weeds
and knocking dirt from their roots,

or pouring tea—those blown scarves,
a moment, more beautiful than the drapery
in paintings by a Master.

—'It is this world of the *dharmas*
(the atoms)
which is the Diamond.'

*

Dōgen received, they say, his first insight
from an old cook at some monastery
in China,

who was hanging about on the jetty
where they docked—who had come down
to buy mushrooms,

among the rolled-up straw sails,
the fish-nets and brocade litters,
the geese in baskets.

High sea-going junk,
shuffling and dipping
like an official.

Dōgen could see
an empty shoreline, the pinewood plank of the beach,
the mountains

far-off
and dusty. Standing about
with his new smooth skull.

The horses' lumpy hooves clumped on the planks
of that jetty—they arched their necks
and dipped their heads like swans,

manes blown about
like the white threads from off
the falling breakers;

holding up their hooves as though they were tender,
the sea grabbing at
the timber below.

And the two Buddhists in all the shuffle got to bow.
The old man told him, Up there,
that place—

the monastery a cliff-face
in one of the shadowy hills—
My study is cooking;

no, not devotion, not
any of your sacred books (meaning Buddhism). And Dōgen,
irate—

he must have thought
who is this old prick, so ignorant
of the Law,

and it must have shown.
Son, I regret
that you haven't caught on

to where it is one discovers
the Original Nature
of the mind and things.

*

Dōgen said, Ideas
from reading, from people, from a personal bias,
toss them all out—

'discolourations.
You shall only discover by looking in
this momentary mind.'

And said, 'The Soto school
isn't one
of the many entities in Buddhism,

you should not even use that name'.
It is just sitting in meditation;
an awareness, with no

clinging to,
no working on, the mind.
It is a floating. Ever-moving. 'Marvellous emptiness.'

'Such *zazen* began a long time
before Buddha,
and will continue for ever.'

And upon this leaf one shall cross over
the stormy sea,
among the dragon-like waves.

Late ferry

The late ferry is leaving now;
I stay to watch
from the balcony, as it goes up onto
the huge dark harbour,

out beyond that narrow wood jetty;
the palm tree tops
make a sound like touches
of the brush on a snare drum

in the windy night. Going beyond
street lights' fluorescence
over the dark water, a ceaseless
activity, like chromosomes

uniting and dividing. And out beyond
the tomato stake patch
of the yachts, with their orange
lights; leaving this tuberous

small bay, for the city
across an empty dark. There, neon
redness trembles down in the water
as if into ice, and

the longer white lights
feel nervously about in the blackness,
towards here, like hands
after the light switch.

The ferry wades now into the broad
open harbour, to be lost soon
amongst a silver blizzard of light
swarming below the Bridge:

a Busby Berkeley spectacular
with thousands in frenzied, far-off
choreography, in their silver lamé,
the Bridge like a giant prop.

One does seem in a movie theatre:
that boat is small as a moth
wandering through the projector's beam,
seeing it float beneath the city.

I'll lose sight of the ferry soon—
I can see it while it's on darkness,
and it looks like a honeycomb,
filled as it is with its yellow light.

Flames and dangling wire

On a highway over the marshland.
Off to one side, the smoke of different fires in a row,
like fingers spread and dragged to smudge:
it is an always-burning dump.

Behind us, the city
driven like stakes into the earth.
A waterbird lifts above this swamp
as a turtle moves on the Galapagos shore.

We turn off down a gravel road,
approaching the dump. All the air wobbles
in some cheap mirror.
There is a fog over the hot sun.

Now the distant buildings are stencilled in the smoke.
And we come to a landscape of tin cans,
of cars like skulls,
that is rolling in its sand dune shapes.

Amongst these vast grey plastic sheets of heat,
shadowy figures
who seem engaged in identifying the dead—
they are the attendants, in overalls and goggles,

forking over rubbish on the dampened fires.
A sour smoke
is hauled out everywhere,
thin, like rope. And there are others moving — scavengers.

As in hell the devils
might pick about amongst our souls, for vestiges
of appetite
with which to stimulate themselves,

so these figures
seem to wander, disconsolate, with an eternity
in which to turn up
some peculiar sensation.

We get out and move about also.
The smell is huge,
blasting the mouth dry:
the tons of rotten newspaper, and great cuds of cloth . . .

And standing where I see the mirage of the city
I realize I am in the future.
This is how it shall be after men have gone.
It will be made of things that worked.

A labourer hoists an unidentifiable mulch
on his fork, throws it in the flame:
something flaps
like the rag held up in 'The Raft of the Medusa'.

We approach him through the smoke,
and for a moment he seems that spectre with the long barge
        pole.
—It is a man, wiping his eyes.
Someone who worked here would have to weep,

and so we speak. The rims beneath his eyes are wet
as an oyster, and red.
Knowing all that he does about us,
how can he avoid a hatred of men?

Going on, I notice an old radio, that spills
its dangling wire—
and I realize that somewhere the voices it received
are still travelling,

skidding away, riddled, around the arc of the universe;
and with them, the horse-laughs, and the Chopin
which was the sound of the curtains lifting,
one time, to a coast of light.

Pumpkins

What in novels is called 'a grizzled stubble'
on these pumpkin leaves.
The leaves shuffle
as you wade amongst them, their bristles
rustling.

One is slowly stepping upon
egg shells,
pagodas of orange peel,
on heaps of tea slops.
And the pumpkin flower,
a big loud daffodil.
You push about darkness, parting the leaves.
A rooster is on this slope, also:
come to peck
outside, in the late afternoon.
It is putting down its spur
with care,
and its eye is flickering about.
The rooster is red
and lacquered as a Chinese box;
a golden hood
down to its shoulders, like a calyx, flexible
upon its body, as it pecks,
flicks,
flicks, and blinks,
pecks. I'm holding one foot up, looking for
somewhere
amongst this vine. And find
the pumpkin—
segmented like a peeled mandarin
or leather
on the back seat of a 30's tourer.
I break the stem
and lift the heavy, warped pumpkin,
just when the vine's become
too dark.
In between pink and yellow,
its orange tone
can be added easily to the sunset
that's been going on.
I put the pumpkin beneath my arm.
Like a bad painting, this magnificent sunset.

The dusk

A kangaroo is standing up, and dwindling like a plant
with a single bud.
Fur combed into a crest
along the inside length of its body,
a bow-wave
under slanted light, out in the harbour.

And its fine unlined face is held on the cool air;
a face in which you feel
the small thrust-forward teeth lying in the lower jaw,
grass-stained and sharp.

Standing beyond a wire fence, in weeds,
against the bush that is like a wandering smoke.

Mushroom-coloured,
and its white chest, the underside of a growing mushroom,
in the last daylight.

The tail is trailing heavily as a lizard lying concealed.

It turns its head like a mannequin
toward the fibro shack,
and holds the forepaws
as though offering to have them bound.

An old man standing on a dirt path in his vegetable garden,
where a cabbage moth puppet-leaps and jiggles wildly
in the cooling sunbeams,
has the bucket still swinging in his hand.

And the kangaroo settles down, pronged,
then lifts itself
carefully, like a package passed over from both arms—

The now curved-up tail is rocking gently counterweight behind
as it flits hunched
amongst the stumps and scrub, into the dusk.

Telling the beads

One drop is laid in each nasturtium leaf,
round as mercury,

and there are several on
every looped frond of the long flat grass;

these
clear sacs of plastic, tucked and full.

Plump, uncontained water,
precipitous,

held together by the air.
They are the most fragile particulars,

on grass that's loping everywhere
in all the trajectories of a flea circus.

Thought balloons,
you infer

that I should begin to fill each of you with an
apt word

which must be of a like transparency.
You are the mushrooms

conceived on the pure walls of the air;
anti-pebbles;

doodlings of a Botticellian elegance.
O *claritas*,

one thinks of lenses, floating upon each other,
dreamed by St. Benedict Spinoza

before a window full of sky,
all the Christians out of the house, and gone to church.

You are the digits of nature's prodigality.
You slip

on these stalks
as if one had become aware of the film

on strained eyes.
Presented on a febrifugal greenness;

someone who hadn't realized a need for refreshment
is made aware of an unventilated taste.

Looked at,
you offer hardly more than that.

This is authentic manna, it contains
no message and no promise,

only a momentary sustenance.
Run the drops from a stalk across your lip

they're lost
in the known juice of yourself, after an ungraspable instant.

Long-reputed but unresponsive
elixir.

Experiencing you, I see before me all the most refined
consolations of belief and thought.

Poem to my father

Dear father, you were buried
     in perfect summer weather.
         Such a day
you would sit outdoors
     and put your bad leg up
         in its slipper,
and pretend not to like it there:
     too crowded
         on the porch, with the pot plants,
or too shady,
     or too hot;
         you would call out
to my mother and sister
     and make them run;
         you'd have your lunch brought
on a tray, with doilies
     and frangipani,
         presented
for you to fault.

Though, some found that day too hot,
     and you could sympathize:
         old-timers
from the R.S.L.;
     those red-faced
         mates of yours, dabbing
with handkerchiefs
     at hat-band welts,
         the purple onion-root
in nostrils,
     cheeks,
         flaring urgently as
heat lightning at night.

I told myself, your father,
     is in the rank grass,
         who gave you body and soul.
That is why I've searched
     anxiously
         your face
propped on the hospital pillows—
     for some trait
         like the corridor
of a dank hotel
     at the end of which is
         hung
a verandah, in the open.

I've found
     such fine bones
         in your face—
you have them yet.
     What one might only wish to keep
         of you, you keep,
also.
     In you, now signifying nothing;
         although
that chemistry was ineffectual,
     always—
         overcome
by some other gene
     or something infancy had done.
         That's all there is to say.

That's all.
     But everything you did once
         we thought against us.
The money you borrowed,
     won with
         and lost again.
All those days you went to get blind,

so well turned out.
                The condemnation
in a haughty voice
        at every meal
                of my books, my hopeless maths,
my choice of sport.
        (I was the eldest
                and had to sit beside you.)
It didn't matter to you there was no
        Rugby Union,
                I ought to be playing it.
I was letting you down.

Who was this
        thin-faced, hollow,
                neurasthenic devil,
with his ulcers,
        at the table with us?
                To whom everything was distasteful.
Mocking.
        How bad-tempered you looked
                after your close
fortnightly haircut.
        I could outrun you, and I needed to,
                by the time I was eleven.

And we ran out
        at night
                when it was past the time
you should be home—
        at our mother's intuition
                prodding
under the lantana
        along the road.
                We'd find you
with the bottles emptied
        that you, already drunk, had decided

you were going to bring.
Once you began
        you'd keep on
                until the blessed, regular
Repat Hospital internments.
        But the day after
                you would get up,
shave painfully, polish your shoes to righteousness,
        and walk in the house
                'looking for trouble';
an excuse for another
        departure,
                to spend the precious
T.P.I. pension—
The Money.

I remember
        our pathetic pride
                to see you dressed again
and walking in the main street
        of that town
                as if you owned the place—
'Such a hide',
        my mother said; she would look angry,
                and almost smile.
We were those sun-browned,
        skinny,
                bare-foot, bike-riding
small animals
        whom you ignored.
                It didn't worry us, for long;
we ran wild;
        we were all right
                so long as you weren't around.

Some might have thought
        you wanted to play the rake,

            yet it was always
without panache—
       with no verve, no enjoyment,
          no gaiety,
that we could ever see.
       With a determined, thin-lipped
         selfishness.
What went wrong
       when you were young? It was nothing exceptional
         that I can find.

So, you will become now
       in your children's lives,
         sometimes,
just the half-conscious, troubling
       sense of something
         we have forgotten to do,
or to bring
       along with us,
         if anything wants to remind us
of you.
       You have gone
         as if you were an illusion.

Although, my mother weeps.
       It is real;
         she loved you
when she could.
       Your second wife, she got religion
         and stayed.
What was going to happen
       to you
         otherwise?
She took in washing,
       worked as a cleaner,
         and got all of us by.
The closest I saw you together,

the most affectionate,
  she was holding your hand
cutting the fingernails.
  You were embarrassed,
   hurrying her.
She wanted to play.
She was then past fifty.

Dear father,
  you did everything badly;
   the most
'difficult patient'
  in the nursing home.
   Poor man,
I cannot believe
  your wretchedness
   on all the occasions I recall.
If I think of you
  I'm horrified—I become obsessed
   with you. It is like
love.
  I am filled with pity.
   I want to live.

MARK O'CONNOR (b. 1945)

Mark O'Connor has been associated with the Canberra group of poets, which included Kevin Hart and Alan Gould, all of whom have trenchantly criticised the Balmain school (or 'generation of '68'). He is an advocate of spelling reform, a worthy cause, but the effect in his work is only to distract the reader. O'Connor is a knowledgeable con-servationist, and his best poems employ facts of natural history and his personal observations of nature to create imaginative experiences. He is widely travelled, and has written much about Europe, but his most striking work is concerned with the Barrier Reef.

In their uncomplicated sense of discovery his Reef poems may be seen as a continuation of the discursive mode in Australian poetry (for example, R. D. Fitzgerald and the 'explorer' poems of Hart-Smith), which sees poetry as a means of conveying information and philo-sophical ideas, as well as emotion.

The beginning

  God himself
having that day planted a garden
walked through it at evening and knew
that Eden was not nearly complex enough.
And he sed:
'Let species swarm like solutes in a colloid.
Let there be ten thousand species of plankton
and to eat them one thousand zoöplankton.
Let there be ten phyla of siphoning animals, and
one thousand finned vertebrate types, from
white-tipped reef shark to long-beaked coralfish,
and to each his proper niche,
and—no Raphael, I'm not quite finished yet—
you can add seals and sea-turtles & cone-shells & penguins
(if they care) and all the good seabirds your team can
    devise—
oh yes, and I nearly forgot it, I want a special place
for the crabs! And now for parasites to hold
the whole system in check, let . . .'

'. . . In conclusion, I want,' he sed
'ten thousand mixed chains of predation—
none of your simple rabbit and coyote stuff!
This ocean shall have meny mouths, meny palates,
meny means of ingestion. I want
one hundred means of deth, and three thousand
    regenerations,
all in technicolor naturally. And oh yes, I nearly forgot,
we can use Eden again for the small coral cay in the center.

    'So now Raphael, if you please,
just draw out and marshal these species,
and we'll plant them all out in a twelve-hectare patch.'

So for five and a half days God labored
and on the seventh he donned mask and snorkel
and a pair of bright yellow flippers.

And, later, the host all peered wistfully down
through the high safety fence around Heven
and saw God with his favorites finning slowly over the coral
in the eternal shape of a grey nurse shark,
and they saw that it was very good indeed.

Turtles hatching

Waiting for weeks till the last one is redy to run, they

break through to evening: the life-race is on.
Winds and oceans that call give no order but one:
'Downhill, fast; when you hit water, swim.' Last

will be picked: so will first. One in a hundred survives.
So they break sand & run, downhill as if cursed.
A perfect break—behind the hill rings with alarms.

(Seagulls halloo joy, ghost-crabs skitter out.)
They are high-revving toys, each wound for his chance.
Swift to seize seconds a brother's corpse buys.

Survivors are movers, deth is an eyeless corpse
on tomorrow's beach. The course is uncertain.
Ten sandy yards to high tide's cool foam, or half

of a low-tide mile over lowlands of rock, pits and
castles of rock crabs; every hole an abyss,
every cross-ridge a deth-lane along which

they must tack to the pass, run in series the gauntlet,
the slaughter-works, crab-lairs; forbidden to stop;
indifferent whether scrambling in sand, scrabbling in slime,

or sculling deluded through sand-pools to beaches of deth.
Caught in cracks they push hard down the crab's throat,
still punting on while life lasts; like wobble-men driven

to toddle downslope, in search of the dark
and lovely reef water, the splash in the in-walled ear.
They are non-stop lether wind-up toys; their limbs

have no setting but *go*. Frendly and clean, with
their lethery touch in the palm, likable as a dry
handshake, a childish pleasure to handle, determined

as cats; this driving downhill force that will reach,
tourist, twice the mass of your coffin, yet weigh,
till it comes ashore, not a gram.

Tweaks the heart, though, to see them seek fate in a crab-hole.
I pulled one out once, wedged and still struggling
down, dropped it with a jerk — a great horny claw

like a parrot's beak had crushed the midsection, sheared
off the hed, and behind moved the armoured tarantula
legs of a hairy scuttler with lobe-stalked eyes.

In pity I gathered a living brother, hiked it over the rock-flats,
(still scrabbling on in my hand) while its brethren, obedient,
filed along moonless crevices, sating ambuscades of queued-up crabs,

laid it down on a rock slope, a foot from the water. It flopped
on straight for its freedom, tripped over a two-inch ledge—
fell and rocked on its back. (A crab darted out, saw my shadow, back-

sidled to shadow.) It squirmed and righted itself, hurried
on (since Nature has taught them to fear no predator
but time, no approach will deflect them), found the slight wash of

a ripple and lost half its weight; then, re-stranded, pressed on, met
the incoming surf of a wavelet, capsized, scrambled up, then
plugged on, hit new surf and brested it well; turned its

flippers to sculling, still floating, too light to submerge;
spiralled a clumsy provocative line, spinnering out
to the moon, lucky with absent sharks and gentle water.

Slipping in, as it left, the shadow, a thousand times larger,
of a parent come shoreward to lay; two ends of the earthbound
process linked in the incomprehensible meeting of kin.

As the small shadow pedalled and bobbed, the great one wavered and slid;
Each followed a line and a speed which by chance had a meeting
when time too was right. Predictable fated concurrence

like the moon and its planet. For a second
the greater occulted the lesser, then as surely
slid on; & the lesser was gone; & my folly rebuked.

Pacific puffins

In October, the pasture-month of ocean,
when the father of gods and planets escorts
the clouded quartered moon, striving home,
on the medow of boxfish and sponge-crab,
targeting on a conspiracy of casuarinas
in the ram of the wind on a darkening sea,
they come to ghost-glimmering islets
smudged under a map of evening stars, to rebuild
the abandoned shrines of deth and birth.

Wing-crash on trunk or tent,
clunk of fethered weight;
silence—and then
the indignant wail of triumph
that whatever puts trees
has less magic than air; then the sharp
home-scamper, heds lowered, furtive as rats;

And the settling, two by two,
in ecstatic down
by the rowdy burrows.

First year finds a mate to canoodle;
second, a patch and a shallow scrape;
third and after, the lone precious egg
is replacement—no hawk
of the air is their master.

This sunrise the season is over. They go
in the dawn-gloved morning bewailing the other pole;
wings stiff as a moonflag; beaks fixed
for precision snatching of krill
in the sprat-doom tip-hooked scissor.

Old salts to whom climates and seasons
are one, aloft on the island eddies
successful, thickening the wind, they pour;
endless as round jellyfish I saw once
on a night-dive, galaxied beyond galaxy
in an infinite regress of size; aloof

and enviable

since words are all we've left of wings.

Frigate-birds

To conquer the globe without flapping a wing
is their dream: buoyed over shoals and sandbars
far as the uplifts of ocean extend
where full spred of wings
drawn into bat-fingered points
grips the pull of air.

Windless they cannot leave ground;
wetted, their oil-less plumage sinks. Air's
their only element. They float
with the standing clouds and eagles.
Below are the oceans, flattened;
above, the infinite uplands of light.
They flop only at night; cannot
waste day; know time is for flying.

Etched out in twos,
the black wings elbow-broken in pairs, redoubled,
show pirate-flag sharp; quiver intense with

a song not seen in crumpled bones
where the wildcat sprang, from
deep vegetable closenesses
of humid green over guanoed soil.

Now poised stretch of wing slides
over faceless Ocean, homing
still homing

upon islands that slide
on the endlessly tossing, recovering grid
under the never-changing stars
of Ocean the Ever-Returner.

Ten minutes they hang on our island's upstream, rigid
till a flick of the half-disjointing wings
has them turned for home. Forty miles away:
they will go at the speed Earth pleases,

hold us still in their view
till a hill locks us out of the sunset.

Orion, to us the lounging summer giant
of Southern sleepless nights, stretches
and points them home, creatures of speed and air
wave-bolstered, sun-lifted,
sea-fed.

GARY CATALANO (b. 1947)

Gary Catalano is acquiring a reputation as one of Australia's more perceptive and creative art critics. In poetry he is a minimalist, perhaps most influenced by the American Cid Corman, and formal precision and refinement are not only the means but also very often the subject of his work. The artist Brancusi represents a particular ideal.

Catalano lives in Melbourne where he was brought up by his Italian grandparents, about whom he has written some moving poems. However, the kind of poem included here seems to us to have more resonance, which is what is required of this style.

Catalano has written two books of verse, many magazine articles on visual art, poetry reviews, and a survey of recent Australian art criticism.

Heaven of rags

The camera, as always,
has caught him
exactly—right foot

extended
to a point
almost the future, eyes

peering out
from a time
always the past. Between

these two points
he lives a thin
eternal life

in this photograph,
a man with no name
and an occupation

hardly pursued. Is it
wholly beneath our dignity
to collect rags, and so

maintain a bond
with a world
always there

a world that records
all its history
in these

pathetic rags?
I should imagine
that the true heaven

is a heaven of rags:
all things aged
beaten and torn

will be there, stained
with sweat and dirt
and basking in the glory

that only comes
of use—old hats
old boots

and the old
crazed skin
of the fallen

a skin so at home
on its body
it cannot

be exchanged
in a heaven of silk,
a heaven of rags.

The river

A wind,
then silence. Pacing
to and fro

in a room
at night, I listen
to the rush

of a river, washing
the whole world
into my ear

a river of air
of ashes
of blood.

No matter how deep
you may sleep
this river

will wake you.
If you bury
your head

in the cool
white mound
of the pillow

the river
will reach you,
your dream

is the river's dream
and your thoughts
are those of the river.

DENNIS HASKELL (b. 1947)

The particular strength of Dennis Haskell's poetry, none of which has yet appeared in book form, is its content; it has an appealing humanity. There is often also an understated daring in his handling of discursive themes. The emotional logic of his work is often impressively mimed by its syntactical movement. Haskell grew up in Sydney, was an accountancy academic, and is now a member of the English department at Sydney University.

The call

A stilled room to which I am called
By an unknown voice, not knowing,
Because of its great stillness,
That it calls from my son's sleep.
In the bush nothing stirs. For once
No breeze grabs hold of the curtains.
Sunk back into his body the voice quietens.
I shift his legs, twisted in the sheets,
Grateful that this sudden nightmare
Has crept back into its own beginnings.
In his sleep I can hold his arms or arrange his breathing
Without objection,
His will gone, sleep
Like the end of an illness.

How we look for meaning in such actions,
As if God's voice called from the centre of our sleep,
But there is nothing: only a silence so complete
Love itself might become a sickness.
What we inherit from the bush is a need for voices:
Myself calling to my son in his recurrent silence.

So I listen again for his voice, or someone's: nothing
But silence come on us as it eventually must
And the need for sound greater than the need for any thing.
'God' is a word sunk deep in the blood, signifying
The certainty
Silence will one day flood our arteries,
The hope for some voice, come
Prowling through our sleep.

Over the tips of the trees, out across the face of the ocean,
Nothing moves.
It is a humid January night with no breeze.
His body is in my hands.

For them no inkling of Time,
Just a simple moment of truth
Without end; punctuated, perhaps,
By a dreamless blink of sleep.

Like the boy clad in singlet
And one shoe who sits for hours
On the lawn, charmed by the grass
Which reappears each time he looks.

Or like the sallow mongoloid
Solemnly tasting the concrete,
Or the one who stares past you
With the whole sky in his eyes.

One could say this is Man unruined,
Sharing the stone's theology,
The vegetable's science,
The meditations of the mouse.

The hospital kangaroos

They are the real spirits of the place,
Having endured a million years
Of bush-silence and bush-darkness.

We see them at morning and afternoon
Browsing through meadowland
At roadside, or brooding beneath trees

Motionless as their own images
Daubed in ochre upon the rock walls
Of pre-history.

In their eyes the apathy
Of a played-out breed, broken
By the monotony of survival.

In their gestures a caution
Sprung less from fear
Than primordial habit. They dwell at the fringe

Of our lives, tolerated
For cuteness or curiosity, prey
To camera and larrikin's gun.

They are the real spirits of the place,
Waiting mutely, year to year,
Like sufferers who perceive an end.

RHYLL McMASTER (b. 1947)

A Queenslander, Rhyll McMaster is now a farmer near Canberra and is
the mother of two daughters. She published one book of poems nearly a
decade ago, but continues to write poetry, and has published short
stories. The sparseness of her output appears to be the result of a strong
critical sense. While she occasionally publishes newspaper reviews, she
has avoided literary controversies.

Her poetry is oblique, quirky, inventive, but restricted in range. It is
distinguished by an original, often almost microscopic observation. Her
work relies increasingly on vivid reminiscence, and most of it employs
the past tense. She ensures that each poem is distilled and authen-
ticated.

Crab meat

We would go down along the creek
which tainted its way, drain-choked, to the beach,
over a sandstung bridge
to where stain-red tins and drums rusted in a bend.
That was where we bought our crab meat.

A not young
woman owned the place—
lived among discarded claws and legs,
rotting carapaces
and a dead sea stench.
Death-clenched or mangled-open claws grew on the drive
along with a forest of dried up
crabs' eyes.

Opening the finger-marked door
we would pause as the breath
from the pots grabbed at our teeth
then reach in, for the crab woman
to say 'More?'

Yes—more sweet, red tipped, white string meat
wrapped, paper-clean, small-packaged by her stalk-eyed
sullen children.

They would scuttle
sideways, gazing at our feet
while we discreetly
ignored the whistling screams
and steam-dim, hot water struggles
of the tossed in victims.

Then, out again,
into the stiff air,
away from the scraped-out-armour carapaces
and the papier-mache faces of the crab woman
    and her brood;

and just think of it as sea food
to be delicately eaten.

The red eiderdown

My head clicked through another frame of pain.
A small steel trigger imbedded in my brain
pressed a shutter on a rigid photograph.

I *was* my head; I was within my head.
My temples bulged with prints and negatives.
I went to lie on the verandah-bed
beneath the warm red muffling eiderdown.
Closed away my mind slurred in an ache
while from the lounge, talk and the sharper laugh
filtered down through feathers and satin spread.

The talk was of the placing of the dead.
They talked of graves and good earth over graves.
The voices spoke of bricked-in pits and things.
The voices spoke of marble mausoleums.

Slipping and rustling in my soft bright cave,
under the cover light as fragrant grass
I listened, placid as a dead one might
yet rose up from my nest, one foot in time
the other in my last wish, my eiderdown,
and stumbling in the dark moved to the light.

Woman crossing the road

It's cold, wind gusty,
I can smell rain.
She crosses toward me
her mouth asking something.

At a certain point
our eyes are forced to meet.
Do I smile?
Wave?
You could take away everything
except the feet
self conscious, steady
edging the pavement.
She moves and looks with care to right and left
('She was run over coming to say hullo').

You could slide all the pieces
out of the picture
except her arms
and her eyes and mouth smiling—
her arms hug her tight,
are posed.

She wants to come over just for a minute.
Half way across now
assured, determined.
(Overhead two crows are fighting with a blue jay)
She says, 'I meant to . . .'
but the backwash from a car fades her words away.

Profiles of my father

1

The night we went to see the Brisbane River
break its banks

my mother from her kitchen corner
stood on one foot and wailed, 'Oh Bill,
it's *dangerous.*'
'Darl,' my father reasoned,
'don't be Uncle Willy.'

And took me right down to the edge
at South Brisbane, near the Gasworks,
the Austin's small insignia winking
in the rain.

A policeman helped a man load
a mattress on his truck.
At a white railing we saw the brown water
boil off into the dark.
It rolled midstream higher than its banks
and people cheered when a cat on a crate
and a white fridge whizzed past.

II
Every summer morning at five-thirty in the dark
I rummaged for my swimming bag
among musty gym shoes and Mum's hats from 1940
in the brown hall cupboard.
And Dad and I purred down through the sweet, fresh
        morning
still cool, but getting rosy
at Paul's Ice Cream factory,
and turned left at the Gasworks for South Brisbane Baths.

The day I was knocked off my kickboard
by an aspiring Olympian aged ten
it was cool and quiet and green down on the bottom.
Above the swaying ceiling limbs like pink logs,
and knifing arms churned past.
I looked at a crack in the cream wall
as I descended and thought of nothing.

When all of a sudden
Dad's legs, covered in silver bubbles,
his khaki shorts and feet in thongs
plunged into view like a new aquatic animal.

I was happy driving home;
Dad in a borrowed shirt with red poinsettias
and the coach's light blue, shot-silk togs.

Tile table

That tile table (paddock size)
would be remarked on now.
Then, it was just 'the table' where cups went 'clunk'
and the enamel pot rang.
So big we all had afternoon tea
along one yellow and green perimeter without disturbing
a central heap of peas (erratic bull-ants in old newspaper).

The linoleum was darker
mossier green,
gloom on gloom tartan to rub a toe along
to trace a pattern of good luck;
(move on darker bars past the scullery hole that smelt
of sunlight (soap) and steel wool in decay,
hop to a lighter edge
past the one-step-down bathroom).

That bathroom housed a bath with white claw-legs.
The cement floor was painted red.
The whole house smelt of ferns, rusted mesh and seeping gas.
The water heater poked its tongue and lit the match.
What child would not be terrified?
'I'm not dirty today,' I lied brightly
covered in fern spores like instant-coffee dust.

One morning (was it just dawn?)
I braved the milk-grey wash of still-night-things,
cattle cupboards, steel uncertainties,
to find my grandma in the kitchen wrapping mounds
of sandwiches.
A woollen ravelled comforter that charged on one battery
she said, 'It's just your Uncle Arthur off to work.'
She put a cosy on an egg, placed toast in a rack.
'Early off is early back.'

MARION ALEXOPOULOS (b. 1948)

Marion Alexopoulos was born in London, and was a school teacher
there before meeting her Australian-born husband and coming to live in
Melbourne. At present she is taking time off from teaching to work on
short stories and illustrations. Her poetry was discovered by Jamie
Grant, who found it outstanding amongst the work he saw in creative
writing classes. As yet, she has only published in magazines.

Lines from a factory

Iris has her hands full
of dead chickens
and her face full of thick make-up
the colour of her name.

It cracks as the day wears on,
wearing off under stress:
the wagging arms and tongues
of overhead machines.

Her cheeks sag
so like the skin
flapped over chicken torsos
ready for the bag.

A vulnerable tower above the others
she doesn't join their conversation;
her riled hands decimate
the corps of birds

dead and denuded.
Iris listens to the radio.
I stand beside her on the line;
we wear protective clothing.

At night I have no arms.
I cannot turn.
By morning they are back. All day they work
exposed from elbow down, forcing chickens into bags.

Fast and rhythmically
you pucker up the bag (like a stocking)
and drawing the chicken's body into yours you squeeze
one into the other.

My mound of bodies never slackens;
I cannot keep up.
I cannot compare with those other arms,
red and violent, tense and always cold.

From where I stand I can see the rabbits being killed.
Not on a roundabout upside down,
but by two men in a side room.
With chickens there is a lot of blood

borne from the slashes by open gullies.
The rabbits die quick:
against a wall
then a scalpel down the length of their bodies.

Sometimes the men wave them at us for fun.
There are no windows here
nor secrets.
Sentience ends.

Night flight

Passengers afloat on many thousand feet
of air.
We hiss like a wind pipe,
tunnel through the night
sheathed in our grey jet.
There are a few lights for readers
propped over satin pages,
others in dental postures
deep in mucousy sleep.
Engines hum to airborne babies.
Outside the wide mouth of blue-black
opens, air-greedy, star-toothed.
My forehead against the glass
caught between worlds,
he comes flying up to touch me.
A hand bridges altitude;
a voice says, 'I am coming with you.'
A dead man swims
beyond the fuselage.

MICHAEL DRANSFIELD (1948-1973)

Michael Dransfield died young, but all of his prolific output has now been made available. He was for a time during the seventies the most widely known of the poets in this book. Since our assessment contradicts that of other recent anthologists, we should perhaps briefly explain it here.

Dransfield, who was educated at a private school, certainly had a striking verbal facility, but his poetry has come to seem mainly an instrument for self-mythologising. This is particularly apparent in two posthumous collections, and is partly responsible for the decline of interest in his work. A further reason for this might be a recognition of the purely fashionable nature of his philosophy, which is made up of hippy clichés. Dransfield's most well-known work is contained in his Courland Penders series, in which he fantasises a privileged and picturesquely decrepit rural Eden, dazzling some, but leaving, inevitably, more and more readers sceptical. We have included some of Dransfield's drug poems as these seem to us less contrived, and they have a moving sense of fraternity and a genuine involvement.

You can't buy much for thirty dollars now

they grow old waiting on a coast for ships which will
never come   they know nothing   they do not know that
    the
past like a wooden warship has gone to the shipbreakers yard

the coast is formed of others like them   they are in strata
the top level has just arrived and the last level is almost
coal now it has rotted and is under a great weight

the salvation army band marches along the shore
their music frightens the gulls

under their clothes they are naked
under their clothes the skin is white like greenland
under their clothes

under the skin countless red tunnels form the perfect net
it catches nothing needs no direction a child can operate it

scabs under the clothes
scabs under the skin
the perfect landscape

how long they wait no-one can guess
sometimes they are on the coast
sometimes the sea devours them

today they are waiting
they are bored   some pace the
length of the day out and some are sleeping

the mother eats its young
the young each other
the sun cannot remain in the sky   the sea is waiting   they
      meet like
lovers in the place of winds   prometheus will know them
      when they come

Two sonnets
For An

in the theatre of the absurd,
digging reruns of a city—
An runs in, lays some
stuff on us; we hit; nod off

watching her fix, blood in the
dropper, blood on her shirt; &
smiling, her at us, at herself,
and her collapse like snowfall.

out later, she makes it with some
straight cat, $20,
connects in a doorshadow,

brings it home, herself, for
all of us, for tonight,
the spaceship rain.

Ric

if we had lots of gear
sometimes, when you were
sleeping, i'd
prepare a shot
tie yr arm, find a nice
veiny place
and fix you

you didn't wake
but when it hit
you smiled a long
sleeping-junky smile
and would say
next morning
i had a groovy dream

VICKI VIIDIKAS (b. 1948)

Vicki Viidikas was born to an Estonian father and Australian mother in Sydney. She left school early, after an unsettled childhood, worked in many jobs, from bookshops to pubs, pursued the Bohemian life in Balmain, and now lives in India.

Her work usually has a frenetic energy and impatience ('My head in my boot / My boot trampling on my future'). It is often in the tone of a passionate rejoinder, and is single-minded in its rejection of all convention (and complexity). D. H. Lawrence was a fundamental influence on Viidikas's work, and she later learned from the American 'projectivists', and from Sylvia Plath. The poems we have included are relatively uncharacteristic in their discursive element, which has modulated their tone and tightened their form. Viidikas is extremely prolific, and there is a large amount of her poetry as yet unpublished.

Ode to a young dog

with her Betty Grable legs
    it's the classical
    pooch stance
    that makes her

eyes rolling upwards
    the pitch
    of her trust

so vulnerable

she's a nude actress
    posing
    for the gaze of a master

    his hand
descending from the clouds
    bearing gifts
    and delicacies

to wholly possess her

she's a pin up girl
    naked
    without a price

    dumb
    dame

They always come

When they have taken away
the childish laughter and dogeared books,
peeled off the last mush embrace,
given the girl
her lipsticks, hair rinses and pills

When they have poured back the drinks
as long as empty deserts,
returned the spurs to the one night stands,
taken off the overcoat
and riddled her bed with song

They'll find
a mirror smothered in lips,
a vacant room with stale cigar ash,
an unpaid bill for a Turkish masseur,
a woman's glove by a handsome typewriter

They'll see
charleston dresses of the mind
with their fringes running like blood,
a list of men's names
from childhood to eternity,
they'll dig the very fluff from the floorboards,
examine the stains on the manuscripts

Which drug did she take?
Which pain did she prefer?
What does the lady offer
behind the words, behind the words?
Their criteria will be:
so long as she's dead we may
sabotage and rape

ALAN GOULD (b. 1949)

Born in England, Alan Gould arrived in Australia as a child. He has
become known as one of the young Canberra poets, his poetry and
reviews having been widely published in newspapers and magazines.
His mother is Icelandic, and one area of his work draws on the history

of that country. Another of his constant themes is the age of the sailing ships.

Gould often employs complex forms, the sestina being a favourite. The surface of his poetry is bluff, dense, compacted, and the tone is usually impersonal. Emotion enters mostly through persona, but it can do so effectively. He has been influenced by Auden's 'crossword puzzle' approach to technicalities and urbanity, and by Murray's connoisseurship of specialist vocabularies. The first two poems included here are unusually relaxed in style.

A change of season

(after a newsreel of a Himalayan spring ritual)

Sleepless on Capricorn;
outside an equinox moon
hangs like a skull's dome
above the orchard where
our peaches and apricots
sweat their sugars; the grass
is electric with reptile movement;
the carnal, murderous traffic
hurtles north through canefields
toward the Sunday headlines.
Inside a fan revolves,
lazily disintegrating
the headlights into cinema
on the roof. The newsreel
of the girl and cobra flickers
back across the decades.
She, an oblation attended
by plantations and film-crew,
has arrived and placed the sweetmeats.
Now from the rock issues
eleven yards of liquid

obsidian, a head puffed
and big as the moon. Last year
a sister died here, her neck
encompassed by these jaws,
her trachea pierced, stifling
a shriek you might have heard
in Tibet, in Brisbane. They sway,
each the other's hypnotist,
a minute, a lifetime, gazing
on the gimlet-eye of death,
till she becomes the cobra's body,
and solemn as a bride, bends
thrice to kiss the lipless
mouth. Thirty years
cannot break the trance,
and we would go as far,
hunched before our screens,
learning to know this vicarious
appetite for darkness,
amazed by the daybreak
that reddens on Capricorn,
on Cancer, where the plantations
tremble their luminous heads.

Letter from abroad

Singapore; a note to say I'm in the pink,
    in love, and imperatrix in what was
a general's house. His orchids, gorgeous, phallic,
    nod beneath my balcony; his pool
delivers me deliciously each morning prompt
    at eight. Then paw-paw breakfast with my Dane,
the paradigm of sugardads—leonine, troppo
    and devoted to my entertainment.

We climbed The Gap, and over Pimm's he pointed out
    Sumatra's breasty coast. The evening sea
behind Shell Island was a burning tray of ships;
    beyond—the Celebean pirates and
the island chain of bamboo alleys, bicycles,
    bazaars. His gaze, (he's been here twenty years,)
was almost native; I (of course) was most impressed,
    and vowed I'd not return to Hamilton
until I'd made each nook my own. This wet equator,
    I could lie and rub myself along it,
purr, and lick its sticky, slackly breathing length.
    On Orchard Road I'm ravenous for what
I haven't seen. The shops devour me, (I may soon
    require another cable—sorry,) *and*
the Sikhs who drive the cabs, so sleepy, cuddlesome,
    not very much unlike the Friday crowd
at Parker's. High rise flats are everywhere and beastly,
    but on the Bukit Timah Road you still
can buy a python by the yard. O dearest sis,
    you can't imagine how I thrive up here,
draconian in my appetites. 'Luxuriance
    becomes me,' so I wrote on last night's banquet-
cloth—which quite put out the Dane. The foreign news
    of course, is sobering, and not three days
ago, we walked along the wharves; and saw them hook
a night-club owner from the harbour's froth
and bandages. The sea itself appeared to sulk,
    and rumour speaks of tribes of millionaires,
of thugs and prostitutes . . . That night beneath the fan
    I did not sleep, and knew the gleaming sea
could lie. So hateful, hateful, yet it made me see
    my death's a chance I never will permit . . .

Anxieties at noon
from **Her four dreams**

It is today; you seem to wake to it,
and sense there's nothing conscience won't permit,
no hazard the adventure won't refine
as light pours through your window like a wine
and islands melt like tablets in a glass;
the sun today will let no shadows pass,
and fiery parrots warble in your ear
excuses that seem rash and cavalier—
there fly your children—gladder to be wild,
there broods that other—he is reconciled—
and there as well the mirror's sudden frown,
but shrug that from you as you do your gown.
Put on the costly Adriatic blue,
put on the mesmerizing necklace too.
Leave by the front, for you are unobserved,
your contact is forewarned, the place reserved.
Now cross the dazzling midday plazas where
the fishermen and frowning soldiers stare,
mount streets of houses heaped like bleaching skulls,
pass panoramas that the haze annuls,
take alleys leading into alleys, through
the parts of town prohibited to you,
now suddenly arrive, and breathless, see
the table that you booked is laid for three,
the place in uproar and the staff, inflamed,
have written out a list in which you're named.
Be cool among the lunches, be serene;
this is the court, and you are still its queen.
The mood is ugly; treat with unconcern
these voices that are speaking out of turn,
this face whose smile you fail to understand,
this kitchen knife appearing in a hand.
This has flared up before; you saw it through

nor will your sweetheart fail to rescue you.
Now turn, to see in white your diplomat;
his limousine is purring like a cat;
his rakish chauffeur, sworn to be discreet
is pissing like a bullock in the street.
You cannot reach his eyes, and other hands
remove you from the door wherein he stands.
Now look away, be free, be unaware
the makeshift surgery those hands prepare,
for somewhere near your throat has just occurred
a change that is both dreadful and absurd.

JAMIE GRANT (b. 1949)

Educated at La Trobe University, Jamie Grant works in publishing. He
is known as an acerbic though always intelligent reviewer, and perhaps
this reputation has inhibited his own productivity as a poet, since he has
only published a shared volume. The tone of his poetry is habitually
one of disappointment and distaste, although he also manages often to
be witty. A poem such as 'Sparrows at the refinery', which is com-
paratively recent, demonstrates an increasing clarity of image and
language.

Sparrows at the refinery

City of steel, where no one lives:
tankers wait like empty hotels

on a bored horizon; in what
could be a model forest—

contrived of surgical instruments
and shiny cans—steam grows like trees

from bitter soil, where nothing
is mortal except the sparrows.

Delicate pipes concealing lakes
of fuel: it aches to spread

its poison rainbows. Oil stored
like anger in the heart's cold

cylinder. Some days I conceive
the mind as a place like this,

hostile and intricate, holding
back the fluid bitterness

of language. Vans tow square shapes
out on the highway. Buildings

on headlands shine. Now morning
starts to breathe, a hiss of wind,

combed by electric wires along
the sea front. Inside my mind

the sparrows coldly contemplate
the ground: each thistle-head torso

as particular as love.

Living out of a suitcase

Now skewers of light
impale the bed.

In the stairwell
a laundry hand

steps quickly on
the fire escape—

and leaves behind only
iron pipes

and stairs, bubbles of paint
on window ledges,

a damp spot
the shape of a sleeve.

Left on the suitcase
an opened letter

explains her altered life:
the house is quite small

but I guess it suits me this way.
The case has joined a queue

of hotel foyers,
diminishing

into the future
like a cone.

Restless traffic outside.
Trace the iron geometry

of pipes—a wall of strangeness
grows behind each

thought. Nothing
to do. Nowhere to go.

*Really, I have to laugh
at myself sometimes.*

SUSAN HAMPTON (b.1949)

Susan Hampton works part-time as a teacher in Sydney and has
published one book of poetry. Some of her work is influenced by the
'word games' style of John Tranter and John Forbes, and by their
sources. We have used her alternative style of poem which is full of
fresh and convincing realistic detail.

The crafty butcher

It's a real old-fashioned butcher's shop
with carcasses on hooks, watch your shoulder,
and sawdust on the floor.
The boy's arms are red-streaked:
he's had his hands inside a cow.
His face has soft white hairs, and while he
tenderly wraps my meat I watch the boss at work.

He reaches to a whole leg on a hook
and slick, neat as an eye in the future,
there's a fingerhold: he tugs the muscle
and begins his craft.

He knows exactly where to put the knife in
and the angle and depth of the cut, and
there's the big knuckle of the knee
and a glistening white thighbone.
A few drops of blood hit the floor,
and away comes the round steak. I reach down
and feel the running muscle
at the back of my thigh, solid as the cow's
which is now hung by the fingerhold
on an empty hook. Don't wince, this
is the craft of the butcher. Look at his face,
those cheekbones, he's perfectly calm
and good at his job.

Then there's just the leg bone with that
glowing knuckle white as the lack of pain
after death, and clean as a finishing line.

Yugoslav story

Joze was born in the village of Loski Potok,
in a high-cheek-boned family. I remarked
that he had no freckles, he liked to play cards,
& the women he knew were called Maria, Malcka, Mimi;
& because he was a 'handsome stranger'
I took him for a ride on my Yamaha
along the Great Western Highway
& we ate apples; I had never met someone
who ate apples by the case, whose father
had been shot at by Partisans in World War II,

who'd eaten frogs & turnips in the night,
& knew how to make pastry so thin
it covered the table like a soft cloth.
He knew how to kill & cut up a pig,
& how to quickstep & polka. He lifted me up in the air.
He taught me to say '*Jaz te ljubim, ugasni luc*'
('I love you, turn off the light')
& how to cook *filana paprika, palacinka,*
& *prazena jetra.* One night in winter
Joze & two friends ate 53 of these *palacinke*
(pancakes) & went straight to the factory
from the last rummy game. Then he was my husband,
he called me '*moja zena*' & sang a dirty song
about Terezinka, a girl who sat on the chimney
waiting for her lover, & got a black bum.
He had four brothers & four sisters,
I had five sisters.
His father was a policeman under King Peter,
my father was a builder in bush towns.
Joze grew vegetables and he smoked Marlboros
and he loved me. This was in 1968.

from **In the kitchens**
Kilmarnock

Square redbrick flats on the skyline of Newcastle,
called after the ancestral Scottish town. Never became
a home, really: it was always a piece of real estate.
The first TV, so life moved from the stainless steel and tile
kitchen to the lounge-room. My five younger sisters
went to posh schools, and I was a misplaced person
with a Leaving Certificate, a few hand-lines, one pair of jeans,
an exercise book of imitation Eliot poems . . . I floated

around unreal Newcastle smoking Viscounts and chatting
to odd solicitors in bars. In her clean kitchen, my mother
was like a storm.

Stockton

So I moved in with Nana, learning to cook
Irish stews in a long narrow kitchen with a smelly
gas stove and cupboards full of dinner sets
brought home by the boys full of grog. Or Pappy,
even fuller . . . but now dead, and so I inherit
a bamboo fishing rod. The breakwater, the breakwater.
I beachcomb or light fires and wait for the tide;
Nana is a pirate with her eyepatch from the cataract op.
We joke like sisters, scoffing brown muscat
with her pensioner pals and talking about who's died.
About arthritis and rheumatism and bad eyes and swollen
legs from falls on footpaths bumped up by tree roots.
I fit in remarkably well, here. I like her friends:
I trim their horny toenails with my pocketknife,
and cut their soft white hair which floats down
between the planks in the back verandah. One day
we empty the kitchen cupboards and wash everything:
a gravy boat, a vegetable dish that belonged to Pappy's
mother; glass soup bowls from the war. A cheese dish,
cut-glass water jugs. I wash the glass on a photo of
Nana at twenty with waist-length thick black hair, and I
say to her, Violet Lillian Gertrude Murphy.
'That's me,' she says. I decide to grow my hair.

JOHN FORBES (b. 1950)

A graduate of Sydney University majoring in English, John Forbes's honours thesis was on the American poet Frank O'Hara. He declined an academic career, and has worked in a number of transient occupations. Forbes edits an occasional magazine, *Surfer's Paradise,* and has published two pamphlets and one book of poetry, the titles of these, *Tropical Ski-ing, On the Beach* and *Stalin's Holidays,* giving an indication of the tone of his work. The poem 'Four heads & how to do them' attracted attention early in his career, and it has become a showpiece of recent avant-gardist writing in Australia.

Forbes's poem 'Drugs' is very much a product of the 1980s and contrasts interestingly with the literary seriousness and self-pity of Michael Dransfield's poems on his addiction. 'Drugs' is an entertaining essay in one-upmanship; Forbes takes us on a connoisseur's tour of drugs, not unlike weekend newspaper tours of the vineyards, but in the middle of the performance admits that his personal favourite is alcohol. There is no self-aggrandising here, nor elsewhere in Forbes's work, which is like an entirely compatible marriage between the melancholy and deflated Philip Larkin and the determinedly cheerful, party-going Frank O'Hara. Unlike many younger Australian poets influenced by recent Americans, his voice and attitudes remain distinctively Australian.

The philosophy underlying his poems is that of an intellectual who wants to assert the superior value of the body, and of an unthinking sensual life — pop music, girls, the beach and alcohol. Some poems remain at the level of mere word games, and we have not represented these; others, such as 'Phaenomena', have real intellectual complexity.

Four heads
& how to do them
The Classical Head

Nature in her wisdom has formed the human head
so it stands at the very top of the body.

The head—or let us say the face—divides into 3,
the seats of wisdom, beauty & goodness respectively.

The eyebrows form a circle around the eyes, as
the semicircles of the ears are the size of the

open mouth & the mouth is one eye length from
the nose, itself the length of the lip & at the top

the nose is as wide as one eye. From the nose
to the ear is the length of the middle finger

and the chin is 2½ times as thick as the finger.
The open hand in turn is as large as the face.

A man is ten faces tall & assuming one leaves out
the head the genitals mark his centre exactly.

The Romantic Head

The Romantic head begins with the hands cupped
under the chin the little fingers resting on the nose
& the thumbs curling up the jaw line towards the ears.

The lips are ripe but pressed together as the eyes
are closed or narrowed, gazing in the direction of
the little fingers. The face as a whole exists to gesture.

The nose while beautiful is like the neck, ignored,
being merely a prop for the brow that is usually
well developed & creased in thought—consider the lines

'the wrinkled sea beneath him crawls' locating the centre
of the Romantic head above the hairline & between the ears;
so the artist must see shapes the normal eye is blind to.

This is achieved at the top of the cranium where the skull
opens to the air, zooms & merges with its own aurora.
Here the whole diurnal round passes through. In this way

the dissolution the quivering chin & supported jaw seemed
to fear, as the head longed for, takes place. The head, at
last one with the world, dissolves. The artist changes genre.

The Symbolist Head

No longer begins with even a mention of anatomy,
the approach in fact leaves one with the whole glittering
universe from which only the head has been removed.
One attempts, in the teeth of an obvious fallacy, to find
the shape, colour, smell, to know the 'feel' of the head
without knowing the head at all. And the quarry is elusive!
If the stomach disappears, butterflies are liberated & while
the head teems with ideas who has ever seen one? Equally,
the sound of a head stroked with sponge rubber or the sound
of a head kicked along the street on Anzac Day could be
the sound of a million other things kicked or stroked.
The head leaves no prints in the air & the shape of an
absence baffles even metaphysics. But the body connects
to the head like a visible idea & so has its uses, for
what feeling is aroused by *The Winged Victory of Samothrace*
but piercing regret for the lost head? And beyond the body,
a landscape is not just our yearning to be a pane of glass

but a web of clues to its centre, the head. And here, like one day
finding a lone wig in the vast rubbish dump devoted to shoes,
the Symbolist head appears, a painting filled with love
for itself, an emotion useless as mirrors without a head.
This art verges on the sentimental. It's called 'Pillow Talk'

The Conceptual Head

1) The breeze moves
     the branches as sleep moves the old man's head:
     neither move the poem.

2) The opening image becomes
     'poetic' only if visualised

3)   but even so
     the head can't really be
                    seen,
                    heard,
                    touched
                    or smelt—
     the Objective Head would be raving nostalgia.

4) Yet the head is not a word
    & the word means 'head'
    only inside the head or its gesture,
               the mouth.
               So the poem can't escape,
               trapped inside its subject
    & longing to be a piece of flesh & blood
    as
         Ten Pounds of Ugly Fat
               versus
         The Immortal Taperecorder
    forever.

5) While anatomy is only a map, sketched
          from an engaging rumour,
   metaphor is the dream
   of its shape—
               from 'head in the stars'
               to 'head of lettuce'

Between the two
the poem of the head is endless.

6) Now the world of the head opens
   like the journals of old travellers
               & all your past emotions
   seem tiny, crude simulacra of its beauty.
   & you are totally free

7)   Greater than all Magellans
   you commence an adventure more huge & intricate
   than the complete idea of Mt Everest.
   And this academy can teach you no more.
                   The voyage will branch out,
   seem boring & faraway from the head,
   but nothing can delay you
   for nothing is lost to the head.

8) Goodbye,
          send me postcards
          and colourful native stamps,
                        Good luck!

To the bobbydazzlers

American poets!
you have saved
America from

its reputation
if not its fate
& you saved me
too, in 1970
when I first
breathed freely
in Ted Berrigan's
Sonnets, escaping
the talented
earache of Modern
Poetry.
      Sitting
on the beach I
look towards you
but the curve
of the Pacific
gets in the way
& I see stars
instead knocked
out by your poems
American poets,
the Great Dead
are smiling
in your faces.
I salute their
luminous hum!

Rrose Selavy

for Julie Rose

> *'a transistor & a large*
> *sum of money to spend'*
> Steely Dan

Julie the beauty of a tooth
& from the red & white checked tablecloth's back garden
     where we're quietly avoiding lunch

                    Julie begins to somersault
O facelift sing of Julie!
O mascara croon!
And Ireland green as hair let every crystal drop of whisky
                              flow to me
    as a fish knife's clatter falling sounds the name of Julie—
              the blue day collects her
              & disappears
Julie breathing like a T-shirt after a swim
              in Crete, Julie
         in Rangoon a Chevrolet Impala
    & in it Julie. She watches osmosis on television combing
         her hair
         & FLASH!
appears like an ice-cream to Fragonard, aeroplane bliss Julie
              helping the air of London get cleaner
         Julie, her watch stopped exact
         sneeze balloon happy griefs
         of the portmanteau
Julie, passing exams
Julie the hand-made spine of rare first editions sunburns
                        under the Eiffel Tower
              Golfball of insomnia!
Julie the wedding dress cries like an Italian face
& when the aftershave factory explodes the Spirit of Alcohol
                        beams on Julie.
Imagine an iceberg's ideal form
or an escaped embrace (!) Avoid such horrors with Julie

              and on a weekend hike with Julie
         the snapshot of a bear!
Julie invites a drop of foam to eternity as a blood bank
                        bursts pulpily,
                   every corpuscle dying in love
                        with Julie,
              more luminous than a burning patio /
                        more tasteful

than a day at the zoo.
Julie, surfing the night away
and in the dark beauties of drugs on the pension, Julie,
a crazed spanner in the intricate works of death!
O bored cigarette Julie!
Julie the myth of beauty where sex is 'concerned'
and Julie the myth of ugliness where helicopters are learning,
slowly,
to dance (their feet are clumsy but tender
tender!)
Even the windscreen wipers on their electric stage swivel
for Julie, even the Enos bubbling in its glass.

More precise than a stocking,
Julie lounges at the pool
she moves like a heatwave in December. It's the year slipping by
it's the strange coast of Mozambique I've never seen—
no it's Julie
buying a blazer.
O abhorrent sunglasses!
I peel an orange listening to the fridge erupt in the night
& in the morning I go to the movies,
with Julie.

Phaenomena

Pellucid stars chart my direction, you who
never hear our intent or voices, polish these
manoeuvers that, by instants, resemble you.
I sketch a course among attractions only to
invent you as a shining vehicle, yet as you
are, I am. Not aridity but removal steers me,
opening each degree of arc to pressure what
fluency beyond you can make exchange for. It

touches your motion as you turn in varied
impressive order, revolving above a space
that closed, still contains you; you create
the elements which we are, the glittering that
responds to you. Your indifference is our
best idea of it. Let me allow its complete joy
to burn in me, as from the grief we blame
you for, may it replace behaviour, the sky over
this catalogue where I trace you out, your
voyages subverted into feeling, as though just
waiting for this did not avoid / what your gravity
will shape in me too slowly & I must change.

Love's body

Certain kinds of knowledge leave the field of
all possible experience, apparently to enlarge
the sphere of our judgments beyond the limits
of experience, by means of concepts to which
experience—even after we've made up our minds
about its blaze of nothing—can never supply
any corresponding objects. So our desire for its
freedom just makes breathing harder and the
effort to get there curves up to the asymptote
of all our energy still available for thinking.
This alone prevents us finding any premiums or
coupons to guarantee it exists in the first place.
Because the thrill of taking off—the runway
lights blurring and the noise increasing until,
without knowing just when, we're in the air—
prohibits their use. I'm sorry but it's hard
enough enjoying a new dimension without
cross-hatching in the shape receding fast
behind us with the line of bright dots
narrowing to fake its distance from where

we are, half aware and uneasy at the way our
thoughts are travelling faster than our words
are formed, as clarity dwindles into the past
and no matter how close we bring the paper
to our eyes, the point will never disappear.
But let's face it, we're not desperately in need
but merely curious to know what's new in the
world and what happens when we touch it.
So a trick would do, if it is a trick and not
just all done with mirrors, enlarging the sphere
of our judgments until our heads explode
with a sudden change in pressure and bits
of false wisdom stick to our faces like bubblegum.
For just as chewing for hours lets you blow
whoppers, to think non-stop, 'If I could just
stretch another inch, maybe a vague idea of its
beauty will leak into my brain', leads on to
amateur philosophy and its enormous evenings
of parlour magic everyone picks up in pubs, or via
cheap paperback guides. This phase of it is boring.
But for the moment rather, relax, watch
the inflight movie or the way the tiny nylon
squares on the hostess' stockings stretch to
rhomboids, or squash up as she moves past you
along the plane. Ask her for a drink or
think of going to bed with her in Tehran or
London, as past experiences fall away like
the memory of their superb engineering and
the gleaming world of eighteenth century metaphysics
opens to your smile and naked body.

Ode / 'Goodbye memory'

Goodbye memory & you my distances
calling love me across the vast golf course

to the greens whose flags no wind will ever ruffle
                    Goodbye memory & goodbye
to the sheets held against the hot windows
on days when the morning's blue intensity so crushes me
I breathe with the gasps of a fat sprinter & only
a teenybopper's crystal sigh answers, so dumbly,
the immense chances the collision of deckchairs
from the briefcase full of words insomnia unpacks endlessly
                    Goodbye memory,
                         Goodbye pyjamas
now summer's cool air will rustle forever against my balls
overpowering like a muscle dreams so rusty no art
is bad enough to do their boredom justice
                    Goodbye memory
                         & the way the mind groans
over its trivia throwing this scrapbook into
the sunrise thinking look how I shine convinced
the day riots because I glance
the mind spoils even the hamburger, training words till
they're all reflex & cooing for torment like a lover
                         in love with feeling his love so pure
                    So goodbye words
                    & goodbye writing, more
ambivalent than a two-brained dinosaur & just as doomed!
                    & goodbye to you, poetry
ludicrous sex-aid greasing the statues of my mind
              Hello the yellow beach & the beauty
that closes a book. Hello the suntanned skin
              & underneath that skin, the body.
                         Goodbye Memory!

Drugs

for Jenni Baker & Simon Bronski

Marijuana lets you know
what you really feel about
this, that, these & those

but cigarettes are just
something to breathe against

while speed wraps itself around you
the way a speeding car
wraps itself around a telegraph pole

and all cough medicine can do
is make it a pure delight
to read the *Times Literary Supplement*

But a wallet full of money
is a different thing entirely

—you know about amyl nitrite,
the Heart Attack Machine?

it's far cheaper than cocaine
& the cat's whisker you can afford

won't give you much of a flash
as opposed to the massive rush
of amyl nitrite's darker hit

So why bother with coke? Rock stars
I don't mean you! But the best

of all is heroin. One day.
One day you'll own a big house.

Then by way of light relief
there's my own favourite, alcohol

which is not really a drug
at all, just as the motto
'lips that touch liquor will never

touch mine' doesn't mean
the girl of your dreams won't be

a problem drinker. Even hippies
will, reluctantly, get pissed

& talk about tripping I won't
because real acid is a thing
of the past & besides I could

be busy, like you are, drinking
which means we both have
a Reason to be Cheerful. Another

is when you're on mandies
you don't need drugs

the body is so calm it could be
a bag of soft expensive stuff

& the brain is as pure
as foam on central ocean tossed
or the driven snow

a girl from Sydney
is hoping she'll find in America

along with the drugs I've left out here
because I can't remember

a thing about them except
they felt like I was swallowing a pill

washed down with a lot of vodka
so that the pill & I both forgot

that we've been mingled
happily ever after. & I've forgotten too

about drugs & music—
how they meet inside you

in pubs & rooms & dances—
blind chemicals to make you freak

or sparkle / rock'n'roll music
to bounce you around.

Angel

not serious about drugs
and into the sky that's
open like a face and
when night arrives the
smiling starts we being
our own stars as the days
pass in their cars and
the stereo fills with mud
we don't care   we walk
in the rhythm of a face
that's awake in the air
and I'd like to kiss you
but you've just washed
your hair. the night goes
on and we do too until
like pills dissolving
turn a glass of water
blue it's dawn and we
go to sleep we dream
like crazy and get rich
and go away.

ANDREW SANT (b. 1950)

Andrew Sant was born in London, came with his parents to Melbourne as a child, and graduated from La Trobe University in arts. He now lives in Hobart, where he is a part-time teacher and one of the editors of *Island* magazine. He has visited England again for extended periods.

Sant's poetry seems very English in its reticence and use of the middle tone of voice. He always deals directly with experience; 'Homage to the canal people' derives from his time working on narrow boats in the north of England. His strength is his interest in and close observation of other people, combined with a classical openness of style and freedom from affectation.

Homage to the canal people

Steered straight into this century I see narrowboats
loaded with coal, cheese, vats of vinegar trailing
a hard century behind them along
the polluted Grand Union, yet their cabins are bright
as their paintings of roses and castles
entering Oxford or Chester, a vivid variation
on a theme bleak and slow
as three-miles-an-hour journeys for boatmen

with more rain than sun
working into their faces.
It's pride that brightened them, and acceptance
that heaven's easy chair was far off as the dandies
composing themselves to ignore their progress through towns
like the arrival of gypsies,
cloth caps pulled down against
complacency. So they denied them a privilege—
their cabin doors closed tight
on china, brasswork and lace
fine as webs slung
across the just-after-dawn hedges, yet
those cabins were no larger than a gentleman's pantry.

Long damp days scattering moorhens
from the pounds, then a staircase of locks,
instinctive manoeuvrings through gushes of water,
hard hands straining on ropes
to steady a full seventy foot boat—
I imagine eyes also twisted
like knots between man and wife
till a good pint could loose them,
could knock over incidents like skittles
and with a brutal laugh set them up again;
that's canal pub community,
a sharing of feelings, an abandonment
with gossip flying so fast it was prophetic,
the boats outside moored with the children
like all relevant history, in the shadow
of the Swan, or the Bird in Hand.

Old woman in apple country

When dusk is approaching
I bring the chair out, and sit—

it's the red vinyl chair
my husband slashed the back of
in a fit, years ago
and I stitched
to make comfortable
after he'd gone. His words
still thunder at me, yet
all the comfort I have was in his hands.
The verandah shades me
from the decreasing light
and the garden has loaded apple trees
he planted, thin whips
of saplings demanding and demanding
those buckets of water.
Occasionally, an apple drops
and I hear his step
on the lawn. But when a car
speeds past, not coating
the trees in dust from the track
I know everything's different—
a hard bitumen layed
across those thoughts. Or else
it's the faces in car windows
reminding me: they are not local.
Noticing me, for a moment
we're each suddenly
foreign somehow, invading repeatedly
each other's difference.
All this happens against
a background of hills
in the cool indifference
of dusk, against which
those apples are hesitant drops
along boughs, the rare light
magnifying their suspense.

Origin of the species

My daughter has captured
wild animals upon sheets
of butchers' paper —

giraffes, apes, possums,
snakes, camels, hippos,
while all afternoon the wind

has shrieked outside like a hyena,
tearing off leaves, kicking
dustbins along the street.

Now her mind is a zoo
that lands an ark
of animals at will;

and they're also free
in the breakfast cereal,
each grinning like a Cheshire cat.

The wind exhausted,
we go outside and discover
a fledgling sparrow on the path.

With 'scientific interest'
I see its tiny bellows-
like lungs won't pump

much longer although
for millions of years this effort
has been relayed.

It will not fly
I tell her; she says it will
and later imagines this

on paper. I bury it where
neither tooth and claw nor theory
will interrupt this perfect flight.

CHARLES BUCKMASTER (1951-1972)

Buckmaster was associated with the group of younger Melbourne poets
who regularly performed their works at the La Mama theatre. His
poetry is intense and romantic, and is also tough-minded and rhythmically adventurous. His theme is the regaining of some rural Eden or
Ur-Welt, and he confronts this constant subject with a stripped-away,
restrained and innovative poetry. Before his suicide he is said to have
destroyed all his unpublished manuscripts.

Wilpena Pound

—Where we had stood
at the peak of the mountain
and had first noticed   that we were
inside.

below us, the pass, and about us
a circle of mountains:
red aside orange
the rocks
laced with colour.

and the bushland below
'so dense, in some areas'

—she had said,

'that one can barely pass through it.'

The Pound—originally,
a depressed plateau, the centre
having eroded, leaving a natural enclosure

—a plain
circled by mountains.

Where we had stood
by the groupings of boulders, inside the Pound

spread on the rocks, exhausted
by the climb

facing west, toward the sun, the miles
of forest against mountain

the isolation!

winding track, below,
through the pass

—the way to the Outside.

Mordor—the mountains—
in the 'other world'.

'This is our home, the place
for our people'

she said,
without realizing . .

'to think that we could
climb down that path, into the forest,
to the centre of the Pound

and never
return again.'

(Taking up your axe—the trees
for your home

. . at some un-marked spring—bathing your child
in the water of the mountains

. . Gardens about your cabin

. . Within the voice of the forest . .)

This circle of mountains!—a natural
and an un-natural
isolation.

'The tribes of the Ranges
were exterminated.' (Poisoned flour,
'Aborigine Shoots'—
'near here, a massacre, in the 1880s.'
said John.

    And for this!—

The Pound stretches twelve miles
—twelve miles of heavily forested plain

thinning on all sides against the mountains.
About and around the centre—the remains of the lost:
where few men have been.
Twelve miles of complete/the final
isolation.

And I had little else to give you but love:
now, there is that which we shall take from you,
this land, being   .
our land:

there is reason for many to be bitter—this land,
your pastures
stained with blood from dark-skinned wounds.

Land of clouds; from the heights of mountain
to plain . .
I go down through the forest and pick up the spear
which fell
from the hand of my brother
as he died

a century past.

Though you refuse our offer; understand, father:
My brothers and I are of the forest
and we are aware of its nature more fully than you

—the forest
is our home father:
the battle to be fought is of self-preservation.

. . And I take up that weapon and return
to the hunt.

Sunset. To the west, etched
in a sky of all colour—a lone tree against light:

and to the north, the Pound: a circle of fire.

KEVIN HART (b. 1954)

Kevin Hart, born in London, came to live in Brisbane at ten years of age. He graduated in philosophy from the Australian National University in Canberra, and now teaches English.

His work, since his conversion to Catholicism, has increasingly reflected a Christian attitude to experience. Hart has published a number of poems translated from European languages and the influence of modern European poetry on his work can be felt in his repeated, stark use of symbols such as rocks, shadows, sun, moon and clocks. He is perhaps the least obviously Australian poet in this book. His work is distinguished by intelligent and rigorous expression and conceptual brilliance.

Nadia Comanechi

Montreal, 1976

Yet there are consolations, she chooses a point
in the hush-swept stadium
straightens arms, legs, attracting us to watch

as, first, she hesitates, then rises—
as if some law
suspended itself to witness her grasp

a point five feet above,
coil, and then unwind, relaxing into mathematics
as a chameleon

darkens to become
one with the earth. Soon, when she lands,
a score will flash,

those leaning against the rails will note
her hair now ruffled,
officials will hear the thud as energy

soaks into the mat,
a pureness will escape, a light from a dying star
or lamp that sheds a curve

across a wall where Rheticus rams his skull
against the stone,
or Kepler, disease crawling through his hand,

drops his chalk,
an abstract love unfolds, inflames his mind,
and thirty years

wrinkle into his face before perfection.
She does not play,
perfection recedes from her, a curve

never to touch its axis:
her instant dissolves, the past expands, she lands
smiling without warmth, entirely human.

The last day

When the last day comes
a ploughman in Europe will look over his shoulder
and see the hard furrows of earth
finally behind him, he will watch his shadow
run back into his spine.

It will be morning
for the first time, and the long night
will be seen for what it is,
a black flag trembling in the sunlight.
On the last day

our stories will be rewritten
each from the end,
and each will end the same;
you will hear the fields and rivers clap
and under the trees

old bones
will cover themselves with flesh;
spears, bullets, will pluck themselves
from wounds already healed,
women will clasp their sons as men

and men will look
into their palms and find them empty;
there will be time
for us to say the right things at last,
to look into our enemy's face

and see ourselves,
forgiven now, before the books flower in flames,
the mirrors return our faces,
and everything is stripped from us,
even our names.

Flies

(after Antonio Machado)

I could never get rid of you
no matter what the room or street:

at meals, kissing my first girl, walking by the river,
you joined me
and now you bring it back to me.

I don't know what minute books you read
upon my ceiling —
the prayers of fallen angels, perhaps —
you sing the song
the radio plays between its channels.

On summer afternoons
when the sun has halved the day's allowance of air,
you dart around
like tadpoles in the coolest water
and make me feel as heavy as my bed.

I've watched your dated soft-shoe act
on blackboards, nuns, and men with picks;
and when, inflamed with Marx,
I gave up God,
you sang of the equality of flies.

But I know
that you have rested on my oldest toys,
upon my Latin grammar,
my love-letters, and my Grandfather's dying face.
I know you live off filth, I know

You never work like bees
and certainly never shine like butterflies;
and yet, old friends,
this morning as I hear your buzz
you bring my past all back to me, like honey and light.

The members of the orchestra

walk onto the dark stage dressed for a funeral
or a wedding and we, the anxious ones, quieten
as we wait to discover which it will be tonight:

they sit or stand before thin books written
in a foreign script, more alien than Chinese,
but its secret contents will be revealed now

as at the reading of a dead relation's will,
for the last member has entered, slightly late
as befits his honour, like a famous lecturer

with a new theory and a pointer to make it clear.
Alas, he too cannot talk except in the language
of the deaf and dumb, but as he waves his hands

the members of the orchestra commence their act
of complicated ventriloquism, each making
his instrument speak our long-forgotten native tongue.

Now one violin speaks above the rest, rehearsing
the articulate sorrow of things in this world
where we have suddenly woken to find a music

as curious as the relation between an object
and its name. We are taken by the hand and led
through the old darkness that separates us

from things in themselves, through the soft fold
of evening that keeps two days apart. And now
each instrument tells its story in details

that become the whole, the entire forest contained
within a leaf: the orchestra is quickly building
a city of living air about us where we can live

and know ourselves at last, for we have given up
our selves, as at our wedding or our funeral,
to take on something new, something that was always there.

A history of the future

There will be cities and mountains
as there are now,

and steeled armies
marching through abandoned Squares
as they have always done.

There will be fields to plough,
the wind will shake the trees, acorns
will fall,

and plates will still crack
for no apparent reason.

And that is all we can truly know.

The future is over the horizon, we cannot hear
a word its people say,

and even if they shout to us
to make us cease
bombing their lands, destroying their cities,

a shout from there would sound like an acorn
dropped on cement,

or a plate on the shelf
beginning to crack.

Acknowledgments

LES A. MURRAY 'Driving through sawmill towns', 'The princes' land', 'The ballad trap', 'Birds in their title work freeholds of straw', 'The pure food act', 'The breach', 'Portrait of the autist as a new world driver', 'The broad bean sermon' and parts 6 and 13 from "The Buladelah-Taree Holiday Song Cycle" from *The Vernacular Republic, Selected Poems*, by Les A. Murray. Reprinted by permission of Angus & Robertson Publishers and Les A. Murray. 'Immigration voyage' from *The Vernacular Republic, Selected Poems*, Rev. ed., Angus & Robertson 1982. 'Machine portraits with pendant spaceman' first appeared in the *Age Monthly Review*.
GEOFFREY LEHMANN 'Pieces for my father', 'A poem for Maurice O'Shea', 'Colosseum', and parts I, III, IV and V from "Roses" from *Selected Peoms* by Geoffrey Lehmann, Angus & Robertson. Parts 20 and 38 from *Ross's Poems* by Geoffrey Lehmann, Angus & Robertson. 'Epithalamium' from *Nero's Poems* by Geoffrey Lehmann, Angus & Robertson. Reprinted by permission of Angus & Robertson Publishers.
GEOFF PAGE 'Grand remonstrance' and 'Prowlers' from *Clairvoyant in Autumn* by Geoff Page, Angus & Robertson. 'Grit', 'Cassandra paddocks' and 'Detail' from *Cassandra Paddocks* by Geoff Page, Angus & Robertson. Reprinted by permission of Angus & Robertson Publishers. 'Bondi afternoon 1915' and 'Country drums' from *Smalltown Memorials* by Geoff Page, UQP 1975. Reprinted by permission of University of Queensland Press. 'Inscription at Villers Bretonneux' from *Collecting the Weather* by Geoff Page, Makar Press. Reprinted by permission of Makar Press.
ANDREW TAYLOR 'Slide night' from *Ice Fishing* by Andrew Taylor, UQP 1973. 'The nocturne in the corner phonebox' from *The Cool Change* by Andrew Taylor, UQP 1971. Reprinted by permission of University of Queensland Press.
ALLEN AFTERMAN 'The real is not enough', 'The ceremony for Mr Najdek' and 'Morning noon and night' from *Purple Adam* by Allen Afterman, Angus & Robertson. Reprinted by permission of Angus & Robertson Publishers.
ROGER MCDONALD 'Bachelor farmer', 'Sickle beach', 'Two summers in Moravia', 'Precise invaders', 'The enemy', 'Incident in Transylvania' and 'The hollow thesaurus' from *Paperback Poets, Second Series 4, Airship* by Roger McDonald. UQP 1975. Reprinted by permission of University of Queensland Press. 'Apis mellifica' reprinted by permission of Roger McDonald.
JENNIFER RANKIN 'Cicada singing' from *Earth Hold* by Jennifer Rankin, Secker & Warburg. Reprinted by permission of Martin Secker & Warburg Ltd. 'Williamstown' from *Ritual Shift* by Jennifer Rankin, Makar Press. Reprinted by permission of Makar Press.
NICHOLAS HASLUCK 'Islands' and parts v and vi from "Rottnest Island" from *On the Edge* by Nicholas Hasluck, Freshwater Bay Press. Reprinted by permission of Nicholas

Hasluck and Freshwater Bay Press.

ROBERT ADAMSON 'The mullet run' and 'My house' reprinted by permission of Robert Adamson.

BRIAN DIBBLE 'Maine' first appeared in *Beloit Poetry Journal*, XXVII, 4, Summer 1977. Reprinted by permission of Brian Dibble.

NIGEL ROBERTS 'The quote from Auden', 'Reward / for a missing deity', 'As Bruce Beaver does', 'The house special' and 'The gull's flight' reprinted by permission of Nigel Roberts.

JOHN TRANTER 'Sonnet 47' and 'Sonnet 55' from *Crying in Early Infancy* by John Tranter, Makar Press. Reprinted by permission of Makar Press. 'At the Criterion' and 'The letter' reprinted by permission of John Tranter.

CHRISTINE CHURCHES 'My mother and the trees' by Christine Churches from *Poets of the Month*, Angus & Robertson. Reprinted by permission of Angus & Robertson Publishers.

ROBERT GRAY 'The meat works' and 'To the master Dōgen Zenji' from *Paperback Poets Second Series 3, Creek Water Journal* by Robert Gray, UQP 1974. Reprinted by permission of University of Queensland Press. 'Late ferry', 'Flames and dangling wire', 'Pumpkins' 'The dusk', 'Telling the beads' and 'Poem to my father' from *Grass Script* by Robert Gray, Angus & Robertson. Reprinted by permission of Angus & Robertson Publishers.

MARK O'CONNOR 'The beginning' from *Reef Poems* by Mark O'Connor, UQP 1976. Reprinted by permission of University of Queensland Press. 'Turtles hatching', 'Pacific puffins' and 'Frigate-birds' from *The Eating Tree* by Mark O'Connor, Angus & Robertson. Reprinted by permission of Angus & Robertson Publishers.

GARY CATALANO 'Heaven of rags' reprinted by permission of Gary Catalano. 'The river' from *Paperback Poets Second Series 18, Remembering the Rural Life* by Gary Catalano, UQP 1978. Reprinted by permission of University of Queensland Press. Both poems originally appeared in *Quadrant*.

DENNIS HASKELL 'The call' and 'For Thomas Hardy' reprinted by permission of Dennis Haskell.

PETER KOCAN 'Retards' and 'The hospital kangaroos' from *Paperback Poets Second Series 11, The Other Side of the Fence* by Peter Kocan, UQP 1975. Reprinted by permission of University of Queensland Press.

RHYLL MCMASTER 'Crab meat' and 'The red eiderdown' from *Paperback Poets 9, The Brineshrimp* by Rhyll McMaster, UQP 1972. Reprinted by permission of University of Queensland Press. 'Woman crossing the road', 'Profiles of my father' and 'Tile table' reprinted by permission of Rhyll McMaster.

MARION ALEXOPOULOS 'Lines from a factory' and 'Night flight' reprinted by permission of Marion Alexopoulos.

MICHAEL DRANSFIELD 'You can't buy much for thirty dollars now' and 'Two sonnets, for An, Ric' from *Drug Poems* by Michael Dransfield, Sun Books. Reprinted by permission of Sun Books, Melbourne.

VICKI VIIDIKAS 'Ode to a young dog' and 'They always come' from *Paperback Poets 18, Condition Red* by Vicki Viidikas, UQP 1973. Reprinted by permission of University of Queensland Press.

ALAN GOULD 'Letter from abroad' from *Paperback Poets Second Series 16, Icelandic Solitaries* by Alan Gould, UQP 1978. Reprinted by permission of University of Queensland Press. 'A change of season' and 'Anxieties at noon' reprinted by permission of Alan Gould.

JAMIE GRANT 'Sparrows at the refinery' and 'Living out of a suitcase' reprinted by permission of Jamie Grant.

SUSAN HAMPTON 'The crafty butcher', 'Yugoslav story', 'Kilmarnock' and 'Stockton' from *Costumes* by Susan Hampton, Transit Poetry. Reprinted by permission of Susan Hampton.

JOHN FORBES 'Four heads and how to do them', 'To the bobbydazzlers' and 'Angel' from *Tropical Ski-ing* by John Forbes, Angus & Robertson. Reprinted by permission of

Angus & Robertson Publishers. 'Rrose Selavy', 'Phaenomena', 'Love's body', 'Ode-"Goodbye Memory" ' and 'Drugs' from *Stalin's Holidays* by John Forbes, Transit Poetry. Reprinted by permission of John Forbes.

ANDREW SANT 'Homage to the canal people' and 'Old woman in apple country' from *The Caught Sky* by Andrew Sant, Angus & Robertson. Reprinted by permission of Angus & Robertson Publishers. 'Origin of the species' reprinted by permission of Andrew Sant.

CHARLES BUCKMASTER 'Wilpena Pound' from *The Lost Forest* by Charles Buckmaster, Prism Poets. Reprinted by permission of Prism Poets.

KEVIN HART 'Nadia Comanechi' and 'A history of the future' from *The Lines of the Hand* by Kevin Hart, Angus & Robertson. Reprinted by permission of Angus & Robertson Publishers. 'The last day', 'Flies' and 'The members of the orchestra' reprinted by permission of Kevin Hart.